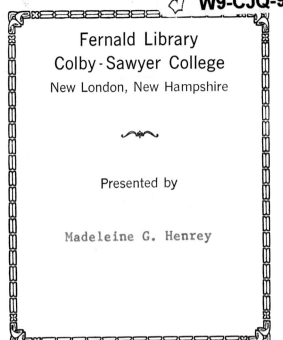

A MONTH IN PARIS

Books by Mrs Robert Henrey

THE LITTLE MADELEINE (*her girlhood*)

AN EXILE IN SOHO (*her adolescence*)

MADELEINE GROWN UP (*her love story and marriage*)

A FARM IN NORMANDY (*the birth of her child*)

MATILDA AND THE CHICKENS (*a winter on her farm*)

A JOURNEY TO VIENNA (*the making of a film*)

PALOMA (*the story of her friend*)

MADELEINE'S JOURNAL (*London during Coronation year*)

A MONTH IN PARIS (*she revisits the city of her birth*)

From a pastel by Honor Earl

A MONTH IN PARIS

by

MRS ROBERT HENREY

For Colby Womens College Library New Hampshire

from

Madeleine Henrey

February 1975

LONDON: J. M. DENT & SONS LTD

Affectionately for

VIOLETTE

Béchet de Balan Neilson

CHAPTER I

I HAVE a tiny room right under the eaves.

Most of the seventh floor of this busy hotel has been reclaimed from couriers and servants who, not so very long ago, used to accompany their masters and mistresses on the Grand Tour of Europe. I am told that it has become extremely rare for a guest to bring a servant. Those who still have homes and servants arrange to do their travelling when their servants are on vacation. Couriers, of course, went out with the family berline. Wealthy women clung rather longer to their personal maids, but now we dress so simply that even the richest, rarest South American woman has no hooks to be done up in her back, hardly anything to iron.

So the rooms on the seventh floor, though small, have been made gay and modern to lodge quite famous people. Paris actresses dispose of their town houses to live under the eaves. My room, for instance, is Bohemian and full of character, and though I have running water and the telephone, I must go a few yards away, as in a private house, to have a bath.

This building is, indeed, two hotels—one delightfully luxurious which I like to cross, coming and going, listening to the high-pitched music of Cuban Spanish; the other modest, truly Parisian, on the roof-tops of the city.

At the beginning, I was always making violent contact with my own roof. I used to bang my head against the slanting wall. I have become more prudent.

I spend hours at the open window, brushing my long

hair, listening to the sparrows. Quite close to me on a terrace, a man is painting garden chairs. I did not see him at first, but a few moments ago when I let down my hair, allowing it to fall heavily down my back, he coughed in a friendly way, without needing to, as if to warn me that he was there, and was looking at me.

I wished him good afternoon and said it was a lovely day, to which he answered that it was precisely because of this, the sun, and the pleasant warm breeze, that he was painting the chairs.

'They will be dry in no time,' he said.

He went on to explain that he would not be there on Friday because there were peace celebrations for the end of the Second World War, and that he would be taking part in one of the many processions.

My window is delightful. I open it lovingly and wide, as I would open a favourite book. Beyond gutters made, I feel certain, specially for cats, the leafy trees of the Avenue Montaigne stretch up like green parasols.

I have just flown over from London. It is five o'clock and at midday I was in Kensington Gardens, but I have already had time to hang up my coat and skirt and take possession of my roof-top home again. I have the curious illusion of still being in the clouds. I can feel my heart, under my white blouse, beating excitedly. The truth must come out. I am deliriously happy to be here again in Paris. I have come to write, to work. Oh, God in heaven, help me to work well, for according to an old hymn I sang when I was a little girl at my Protestant school, there is no happiness without work.

My friend Georges Marin who is captain of The Plaza-Athénée, this great vessel moored to the Avenue Montaigne, rings me up to inquire if I made a satisfactory journey, and if I have had time to notice that the chestnut-trees are in flower all the way along the Champs Élysées.

'Springtime in Paris!' he says. 'Shall I take the car and drive you as far as the Étoile?'

'Yes, indeed. That would be lovely.'

So here we are in the glistening sunshine of this Sunday evening, driving slowly along the wide avenue with the wind-screen down so as to catch every refreshing breeze.

'Tell me some exciting news,' I say, settling down comfortably.

'Political?'

'No, of course not. About those lovely Latin American women, for instance, who intrigue me so much as they cross your foyer in a cloud of perfume.'

'They are delicious,' he answers thoughtfully, 'joyous and intense but quick to fly into a temper, as only women as lovely as they have a right to be. They drive our chambermaids crazy. It is very difficult for a chambermaid to go to an apartment several times a day and to tidy it up without disturbing too much what is lying about. You must have gone down an hotel corridor a hundred times and seen the chambermaids bunched together in the room marked "Service." From here they watch the comings and goings of the guests. The lady and the gentleman from the apartment opposite have just gone out. Immediately the chambermaids with their pass-keys will slip into the apartment to note with expert eye what sort of tidying up requires to be done. The bath-room will come first: the chambermaids will put clean towels on the hot rails. After this they will attend to the bedroom.

'There is a mountain of tissue-paper as high as Mont Blanc. These guests are South American, young, and desperately in love. They must be on their honeymoon.

'Everybody in the room marked "Service" has already noticed the halo of LOVE which surrounds this good-looking couple. They are all interested, pleased, even a little thrilled. Then again, lovers are generous. Lovers pass quickly down the passage, blind to all around them, their hands clasped. When the valet comes back from taking the shoes to monsieur, he reports: "Anybody can see that the lucky fellow is just head over heels in love." The chambermaids think that SHE is pretty. They have seen her in the lace-trimmed *déshabillés* she bought the other day. They take turns to come in when she rings, to bask in the atmosphere of a young woman beloved. They pretend in her presence not to look at her but they have even noticed the beauty spot on her right shoulder. SHE was sitting in front of the mirror, doing her hair. They saw the reflection clearly.

'What I am leading up to is that every morning they went shopping and every afternoon more dress-boxes and hat-boxes were strewn about, the mountain of tissue-paper grew taller, but as they were on the point of leaving to spend a week in Rome before returning to South America, the clothes had to be packed and the paper and boxes thrown away. At the last moment came three new hats in three gay hat-boxes tied up with ribbon, and across the boxes one could read the name of the most famous modiste in Paris.

'Madame immediately put one of the new hats on her pretty dark head, and as monsieur exclaimed that the hat was delicious and that she was adorable, madame decided to keep it. So she tossed the box away, with all the other rubbish, and went off with monsieur for a last dinner in their favourite restaurant at the other end of Paris.

'The chambermaid, coming in to tidy the bedroom, faced once again with a new mountain of tissue-paper and more boxes, took everything up in her arms, threw it away, and set about tidying the apartment. She changed the towels in the bath-room, drew the curtains, turned down the bedspread, and giving a last satisfied look round, murmured:

'"They can come back whenever they like. The nest is ready."

'The next morning was their last. They would have lunch in the hotel and take things easily before catching the Rome Express. Their sleepers were booked, the bill was paid, and madame was gayer than ever, twittering like an exotic bird, laughing, dabbing perfume behind her pretty ears, looking quickly into each mirror as she passed to catch reflections of her shining black hair with its deep blue shimmer. Some might still like blondes, but the valet, the chambermaids—and her lover—were all of the opinion that she was a perfect South American brunette.

' "My darling," she said (in Spanish), "I can't think what I've done with those two little hat-boxes—the ones that arrived for us yesterday."

'Feminine premonition that she might need a little male help cause her to employ the "us."

'They looked everywhere. They rang for the valet and the chambermaids but there had been so many hats, so many boxes! Madame burst into tears. The chambermaids were at their wits' ends to know what to do. The director must be sent for.

'And so,' says my friend M. Marin, as we drive slowly under the pink and white chestnut-trees that garland the Champs Élysées, 'I arrived on the scene like King Solomon with everybody expecting me to show forth my wisdom. The lady was so pretty and appealing that I could not stand by and allow her to cry. I remembered the aridity of our prisoner-of-war camp at Colditz. I am tired of harshness. My heart melts when I see a woman in tears. I am not even shocked when a pretty woman is a little spoiled. No, I am charmed, and I wish there were no greater tragedies in life than two pretty hats gone astray.

'My South American brunette was a real pretty sight! Of course, she was angry, but is there any difference between an angry butterfly and a happy butterfly? No, they are both merely butterflies and a man would have to be a beast not to enjoy the sight of both. I calmed madame, and hurried to my office where I telephoned to the most famous modiste in Paris, who said to me:

'"There is nothing to worry about, Monsieur Marin. I will turn every girl in the place on the job. You will have two new hats within an hour."

'"But whatever you do," I pleaded, "make sure that they are the right hats. Don't remake the hat that survived the disaster. I will try to describe this one to you. It is perched unhappily on the top of the ormolu clock which, incidentally, does not work any more. You know what these antique clocks are, but they look nice in hotel suites. Ah yes, the hat. Well, I would call it a flowered thing. Primroses, perhaps?"

'"Everything is quite clear," said the famous modiste at the end of the wire. "I see it all now. We must remake the one with the ribbon and that other little straw hat with the cherries; and in an hour, Monsieur Marin, in less than an hour, everything will be all right again. We shall send one round first, and then follow it up with the other. Your little South American friend will just have time to dry her tears and smile again. At her age tears leave no lines on the face."

'The hat with the ribbon arrived in time for madame to wear it on her journey,' M. Marin says proudly. 'The other took rather more time than we expected, but I rushed it to Orly and it went to Rome by air. They found it at the hotel when they arrived. I don't think this small delay could have mattered. After all, she could hardly have worn it between here and Rome, could she? Really, don't you think Paris looks lovely?

'As you will have gathered,' says M. Marin a moment later, as if he had turned the question over seriously in his mind, 'I don't know much about women's hats. I know about soldiering, and horses, of course, but what I like here is the unexpectedness of each situation. My staff is very helpful. They all have my permission to wake me up at any hour of the night. Situations are often as piquant as those we read about in eighteen-century literature.

'The other morning, very early, a man rushed into my office and said: "My two sons have not been back all night. This morning when I went into their rooms their beds had not been slept in. Oh, my sons! My poor unfortunate children! In this city of vice they may well have been kidnapped or murdered!"

'I was not very pleased to hear Paris described as a city of vice. I could have pointed out that Paris is no more dangerous for two young men than Buenos Aires, London, or Chicago, but I told this wealthy and im-portant South American that there was only one thing to do, and that was to telephone to the police.

'But though a moment ago he had feared that his sons had been murdered, he took it as an insult that I should want to ring up the police.

'But while he wiped his brows with a white silk handkerchief, I rang up my friend the Chief Inspector who very quickly informed me that the two bad lads were locked up on a charge of disturbing the peace in a night-club and using insulting language to a police-officer.

'"I'm afraid it's quite serious," I said to the father. "Drunk and disorderly, and insulting the police."

'"Oh!" he exclaimed, giving a big sigh of relief.

"If it's nothing worse than that, I shall be able to tell my wife the truth."

"'I don't mind going round with you to police headquarters," I answered.

'The Cadillac drew up at the hotel entrance, and the uniformed staff saluted as usual. The page-boy opened the door of the car wondering what I was up to with a flustered-looking guest at this early hour.

'I would not have you believe, Madame Henrey, that my uniformed staff is inquisitive in the real sense of the word. They are interested. It is their job to be interested. They register mentally each coming and going, and what is said and done, so that later when I ask them "Have you seen M. X or Mme Z?" I am told exactly.

'I gave an imaginary address to the driver, and as soon as we were out of sight, I tapped on the window and said: "Police headquarters." I knew that on our return to the hotel the chauffeur, who is an excellent fellow, would tell all the other chauffeurs, my porters, and even the page-boy where we had been, but as the indiscretion would not be mine, I could wash my hands of it.

'The Chief Inspector was delightful. He sees so many different sides of life. Everything that happens nocturnally in Paris comes before him like a film the next morning. With the South American, who kept on mopping his forehead, he was dignified and severe. To me who am his friend, he said:

"'They are a couple of young rogues, if you ask my opinion, and are lucky to come up against an elderly mustachioed *sergent de ville* who has sons of his own. All the same I was for giving them a lesson and so I sent them in the Black Maria as far as the Petite Roquette. Your customer might like to go and see them there. I'll make you out a pass."

'So we went to the Petite Roquette where we found them without belts, without ties or shoes, a good deal sobered up. But I must say they were delighted later when, after appearing in court with a barrister who had been pining for a job to defend them, and being released with a caution, they returned to the hotel.

'"We enjoyed ourselves tremendously," they said, "being in prison with amazing people, real thieves, real burglars. We would never have seen so much of life by merely going to a night-club."'

CHAPTER II

I WAS BORN in Montmartre but I have never been to the Comédie Française. The heart of Paris was another world for the little girl with pigtails who sewed so diligently at her mother's feet. After that I became a Londoner by marriage and assimilation.

I am resolved this spring in Paris to do all the things that I have wanted to do. I want to see those plays in the repertory of the Théâtre Français which, in the course of my literary education, I have read a dozen times. I want to saunter beneath the windows of the Palais Royal. I want to walk alone through the streets of Paris, even perhaps at night, which, in any city, for a woman, is a difficult thing to do. We who are women do not normally go out without a reason. We go to work (if we have to), to the hairdresser, to call on a friend, or to buy a yard of ribbon, but we do not go out merely to observe. We are not free in that sense. If we go to the theatre, somebody else chooses the play. I want for a moment to do what every woman dreams of, to enjoy the illusion of complete independence.

A powerful friend at whose lovely house I lunch says to me when I tell her all this:

'They are doing Marivaux's *Le Jeu de l'Amour et du Hasard* at the Comédie Française, and Mlle Hélène Perdrière carries off her part with sweet, flustered anxiety. But first, to have an idea of what our modern Paris apartment houses look like, you should see her at home. I must arrange it.'

Mlle Perdrière lives in a blinding white apartment house near the Trocadero. The tenants buy their flats. It is the new idea. She opens the door herself—small, blonde, absolutely lovely with an adorable nose. She has just come back from a South American tour, and has been prodigiously interested in the Argentine, where the players arrived as Mme Péron was dying. And they were billed to play *La Reine Morte*.

'Bitter discussions milled over our heads,' she says. 'Some would have hastened her death; others spoke of her as the greatest woman of the age. But whether people spoke ill of her or well, they talked of nobody else. The women were jealous of her, for she dressed fabulously. We were told of her last great mass meeting where she addressed the crowd in her loveliest furs and diamonds. To hecklers, she cried: "I have been as you are, and this is how I am. You can become as I am if you want to." It was true in a way, and wonderful for the women in the audience, but on the other hand how many of them had her amazing beauty and her gift of oratory? At all events, we heard so much about her that we also became interested. She seemed the whole spirit of the Argentine.

'We worked very hard, we rehearsed, and we tried to do a little shopping. The Calle Florida was full of rich American cars. The women I thought magnificent, with the sort of jewels that make one dream. The night she died all the theatres closed. I have never witnessed such amazing scenes. Women wept in the streets. They were jealous of her during her lifetime but she was a woman loved by women, and that's a pretty rare thing.

'Later the crowds filed before the body. There were thousands upon thousands of people but the ambassador helped us to pay our respects. Her features made a tremendous impression on me. Her hair had been bleached to make her blonde, but because she had been ill for quite a time the dark roots had been freshly dyed so that she would appear to the people in all her loveliness. What surprised me most was the length of her lashes, and their thickness. They looked like the lashes of some expensive doll. I was told that it was due to hormones. Then again her hands were of rare beauty. I could not take my eyes off them. The women, tears streaming down their cheeks, bent down and kissed the hem of her dress. Do you know what strange thought came to me at this moment? That I was living in some past age, watching something out of our repertoire, and that instead of being strolling players, we were the audience of a medieval play.'

That same evening I am in Hélène Perdrière's dressing-room at the Comédie Française, and now, as the actress about to go on, she is in a magnificent dress of straw yellow faille. And what strikes me most about her is the slimness of her waist. Her waist is adorable, the curved, doll-like waist that often proves the triumph of the small woman. Then again there is the Madame Pompadour wig, so evocative of the past and yet so extraordinarily modern.

'Ah!' she says, after listening sweetly to my enthusiastic compliments, 'I am not really quite satisfied with my wig this evening.'

'What would I give,' I answer, 'to dress my hair like that. How happy I would be!'

There is a light knock at the door and an elderly man wearing a white apron comes in. Hélène Perdrière allows herself to be examined. He looks critically at every angle of her pretty head.

'As you took so long to come this evening,' she says sweetly, 'I crayonned the three black spots on my nape.'

'They are satisfactory,' he says.

This elderly man is the genius of wigs and hairdressing. He has the strict, critical eye of a king of France for the coiffure of a lady in panniers, but he also knows how Helen of Troy dressed her hair, and how women looked in Alfred de Musset's time. He has a way of blowing lightly on a coiffure to give it sparkle, like those little gods on old maps blowing with rounded cheeks into the sails of a ship to send it riding across furrowed seas. When you and I, on the threshold of important occasions, look at our hair, wondering what we can do to set it alight with glamour, and sometimes because everything appears wrong, give way to nerves, this expert of past and present resorts to veritable magic. He has a dauphin, a sort of Prince of Wales, who follows him at a respectful distance, but the great king of the comb has such deftness and speed in every movement that the poor dauphin is hard put even to see how it is done.

We are on the third floor—a long corridor running in a half-circle, with famous names meeting the eye at intervals, and here comes a group of Greek shepherds who, having played in *Pasiphaé*, smoke a cigarette before taking off their shepherds' clothes.

Hélène Perdrière and I hurry down. A door opens. Here is Gisèle Casadesus who exclaims:

'Oh, my little Hélène, I've got the jitters terribly to-night.'

'And so have I,' says Hélène. 'I always have them with Molière or Marivaux. Comedy is far more difficult than tragedy—wave after wave of sparkling, rapid wit, breaking sequence upon sequence off the tip of the tongue!'

Then turning to me:

'Like Sheridan but multiplied by two!'

We laugh happily, youthfully, for I can see that she is not really frightened; but now we are caught in the glare of naked arc-lamps and the staircase, having become wider, has a worn red carpet and a mirror which reflects—a slim woman in a tailor-made whom I recognize almost with a shock as myself, and two actresses about to play Marivaux whose rich dresses swirl round them in a continuous and delightful frou-frou.

There, in front of us, is a man!

If the Louis XV costumes are becoming for women, they are even more so for men. My goodness, what a lovely looking man! My heart beats faster and I am absurdly ashamed of my narrow, short skirt. I must look terribly queer. If it were not for the occasional mirror that throws my reflection back at me, chiding me, the illusion would be complete. I would be living happily in the eighteenth century.

But here are more Greek shepherds hurrying towards us. M. de Montherlant's play is finished, and there is a thunderous roar of scene-shifting as the stage is prepared for Marivaux.

I must leave my friend and join the audience through the pass door.

The curtain goes up and I am back in the days of Louis XV.

I almost feel ill with delight at the sound of this lovely French which we moderns take such pride in degrading. What tender reminders of love are present both on the stage and off it in this city of Paris! What a satisfying atmosphere for a woman!

On my way out I go up into the long gallery where the authors whose works are played at the Comédie Française are represented. I look for my idol. I fear for a moment that I will not find her. There she is, that great woman amongst so many great men—Alfred de Musset, Théophile Gautier, Balzac, Sandeau.

She sits on what looks like a little throne and her foot is bare. I am very moved by the sight of this statue

which Clésinger made when he came to Nohant, breaking the hearts of two women, causing the death of a
third.   Did he not marry Solange, the writer's daughter,
make her unhappy, and then take away their little girl
who caught cold and died?

But the statue which Clésinger made is beautiful.

I bend down and kiss the toe, having long dreamed
of paying this tiny mark of my respect to the great Mme
George Sand.

CHAPTER III

COCKTAIL-TIME in Paris, during those feverish, agitated hours before dinner, is for many women the most dazzling moment of the day, for it brings the sexes together in equal strength, and forms a propitious setting for fashion, conversation, and love.

I do not need to go any further than the bar of what in Paris is my home—The Plaza-Athénée. The world gravitates to me. I am dining to-night with a very important American and a young French couple. SHE creases up her eyes to look at me as we are introduced. SHE is blonde, tall, and elegantly slim. SHE asks me about my son, then talks to me about her own.

The tables are so close together that it is a great wonder that the barmen can thread their way between them, and then everybody is always getting up and sitting down. A gentleman, for instance, rises from his chair at an adjoining table and with a charming bow kisses my companion's hand.

'Oh!' she says, as soon as he has gone off to pay his respects elsewhere. 'He is really a most amazing person, a wealthy bachelor who very gaily spends his capital. He gets up very late, only starting to live at cocktail-time. One sees him in all the fashionable night-clubs, for he is an enthusiastic and beautiful dancer, and dances regularly till 4 a.m. When I came across him yesterday at the Law Courts it was the first time I had seen him by daylight, and I was startled to notice that he was as white as chicory.'

'In the Law Courts?'

'Why, yes, he was involved in one of those foolish quarrels between individual owners of an apartment house.'

'And you?'

'I? Alas, my case was more serious. A love story. . . .'

'A love story!' I exclaim.

'No, no,' she says quickly as if to warn me that it is not a gay love story. 'I had a great deal of unhappiness.'

She smiles rather sadly.

After dinner we go down the Champs Élysées illuminated from end to end. What a magnificent sight on this warm evening! The sidewalks and the café terraces are packed with people. My young friend says to me:

'When I see Paris looking like this I don't mind a bit never going abroad.'

Our American host is driving us slowly in his large Cadillac, the young husband beside him, the young wife and myself behind. My companion exclaims suddenly:

'I mustn't forget I left my own car standing outside the hotel!'

Then, in an explanatory way, to me alone:

'I have one of those small cars that the young married women in Paris all have now. We women have come to consider a car as part of a normal wardrobe, as necessary to our existence as our hats, shoes, and dresses. We drive the children to school, fetch them in the afternoon, and go to the hairdresser. The trouble is that I am short-sighted (I expect you notice how I screw up my eyes to see things) and I often mistake somebody else's car for mine. The other day, for instance, I took the key out of my hand-bag, opened the car, and drove off. I had almost reached home when I suddenly caught sight of a man's hat on the empty seat beside me.

Hurriedly I turned the car round, drove to my starting-point, put the car where I had found it, and took my own. I was lucky. I might have finished at the police-station. That's the trouble when so many people have cars which look exactly alike!'

Oh, what a pretty dress she is wearing! I am furiously jealous. Mauve, but more the mauve of lilac than of wisteria, and the skirt so cleverly pleated that she looks as if she was dressed in a fan, and this makes her slim waist look even slimmer.

'No,' she says in answer to my query, 'I did not buy it from a famous dressmaker, but I found the material and had it made up by a woman. The material and the cost of making it up worked out at thirty pounds. Well, I suppose it is expensive, but it's the sort of dress one can wear either at a very smart evening party or at an afternoon reception, and then once in July in the Bois de Boulogne. In August when we go away for the holidays, I shall finish it at the Casino. As a matter of fact I am already thinking about what I shall need for the autumn, aren't you? Fashion changes very little just now, but all the same—that does not prevent us from wanting to have new dresses, does it?'

What delights me most is that Parisian women are abandoning their flat heels. The ballerina shoe is on the wane, and it is a miracle to see women who a year or so ago walked with the long strides of a gleaner, now perched on high heels that are new and lovely in the extreme. They are not only very high but so delicately fine that they give the impression of narrowing to nothing. I look out of the car window to watch with a strange thrill a woman crossing the Champs Élysées (a tremendous achievement in itself) perched on heels that are simply fairy-like. The base is certainly not larger than a sixpence. Never should I be able to dart through traffic on heels like that. I should break my neck. But the sight of them worn by so many women fills my mind with a furious desire to have the same, and soon I can think of nothing else. The young, and even the less young, look like Winged Victories.

Oh, and the hats!

Manet, when painting, used to say that there was nothing so difficult as to balance a hat on a woman's head. The Paris modiste and the Parisienne do not share that opinion.

How the love of Paris begins to run in my blood again!

I have twice crossed the Champs Élysées to-day, but as I was merely wearing London heels perhaps that does not count. I cannot yet call myself brave.

There are the most adorable shops kept by artisans all round the Avenue Montaigne. They are so small that they never appear either to open or to close. They are full of fascinating things. A newsagent in the rue Clément Marot reminds me of some quiet village in the Loire. I buy a newspaper and two ounces of knitting-wool. The old lady scurries mouse-like from the newspaper counter to the haberdashery counter. She might be playing musical chairs.

I take a dress to be cleaned at the shop next door. The price, compared with London, seems so high that I wonder if I would not do better to take the dress back to the Avenue Montaigne and clean it myself with benzine, but the woman says sweetly:

'Madame, your dress will be so pretty when we have finished with it! I will iron it carefully and you will be proud to wear it.'

Three little girls in red cardigans and bedroom slippers play on the pavement. They skip lightly, then suddenly exchange secrets, breaking into girlish laughter. The roads are paved and bear the names of famous men of the fifteenth and sixteenth centuries, Marot, the poet, Montaigne (who harbours my hotel and Christian Dior), the celebrated essayist, friend of Mlle de Gournay.

Now here is the most picturesque shoemaker!

His shop front, not more than a yard wide, enchants me. Oh, but see these adorable high heels of the very same kind that for the last twenty-four hours have made me ill with envy! They are utterly beautiful, and my heart beats violently against my ribs. This man does not apparently sell ready-made shoes. He makes them to order, which will give me an excuse to look at the ones in the window, to take them up in my hands, without being tempted to buy them. Then also I will be able to inspect this little shop that Marot could surely have sung. It is a sixteenth-century shop in a twentieth-century city. There! I have pushed open the narrow door, and walked in! Tiny indeed is the shop, but a corkscrew staircase leads down to a basement from which comes the sound of light hammer blows.

A small man with a light linen apron, stained with wax in places, arrives and bids me good day, his eyes turning professionally to the shoes I am wearing.

'Sit, sit, little madame!'

His language is strange, affectionate but respectful. He moves about his shop with such sure knowledge that he does not bump up against the walls. But of course he has ready-made shoes! I am filled with alarm. I shall never have the heart to disappoint those large dark eyes.

'No, no,' he says as I take the shoes out of the window. 'Not buy those. Not pretty enough for little madame. These much more pretty. See, little madame!'

And he holds in his work-roughened palm a shoe worthy of the Greek courtesan Rhodopis.

'But the heel is so high it will kill me!'

'Not too high for you, little madame. Very comfortable. Very stable. You will be surprised. Think that if we killed our customers or made them ill, we would have no more business. Sit, sit, little madame. You will try.'

They are blue and white, soft as a glove. I have them on. I am filled with unspeakable joy. My shoemaker tells me he is Greek and cannot make himself think in French.

'Always I think in Greek and about shoes,' he exclaims, laughing. 'I will make you all your shoes whether you are in Paris, in London, or in New York.'

Perched on my high heels, I trot delightedly back to the roof-tops.

What a wonderful day!

CHAPTER IV

HAVING WORKED, as I always do, till midday, I do my hair, dress carefully, then fly into the sunshine of another beautiful spring day. The trees spread green freshness over the scintillating exteriors of chauffeur-driven cars. The sidewalks are wide, cool, and inviting. Paris burns and agitates but I have no appointment. My heart responds to the joy of absolute freedom. I walk as far as Fouquet's, choose a table on the terrace, and order black coffee and a roast beef sandwich.

The superb spectacle of the Champs Élysées vibrating, screeching, flashing, takes place all about me. No colours are more piercing than these under a bright sun. The waiter brings me a small plate, a knife and fork, a great assortment of mustard pots, and a long piece of golden, crusty French bread from the sides of which emerge delicious slices of underdone beef.

A girl detaches herself from the two-way stream of passers-by and inspects the café terrace. She cannot see the person she obviously hopes to find, and so she sits down at a table to wait for him. How very amusing! I shall, unknown to her, wait for the same person as she is waiting for. We shall wait together. I am thrilled at the idea.

She might be an English girl, for she is tall and reminds me of the girls portrayed on the outside of my English women's magazines. She is a trifle overdressed, wears her hair in the poodle style, has earrings, a necklace, and bracelets. Hardly is she seated than, feeling the heat, she unfastens the zip running down the

front of rather a pretty corduroy lumber jacket, and
takes it off.   She is now in a white blouse with large,
important sleeves that reach to the elbows.   Her black
skirt, very tightly fitting, with high pockets, is made in
one of these mysterious new materials I can never quite
be sure of.   Her lack of hips gives her an almost boyish
line but she has beautiful long legs.

Her features are strange.   She is only a girl but
there is a good deal of experience written in her face.
She is youthful chiefly in age.   Is she Swedish?   For
though she has not yet opened her mouth, I have
decided that she is not English after all.

Her eyes are deeply blue, her cheeks of a natural and
delicate pink, and this double manifestation of purity
and girlishness seems merely to accentuate the clash
between youth and experience.

She is extremely worried.

From time to time she turns to give a sweeping look
along the café terrace to make sure that the person she
is waiting for has not arrived, and when the waiter comes
to her table, she throws him a brief command: 'Perrier
water!' as if anxious to get rid of him.   I can almost see
the mounting excitability of her nervous system, and
tiny circles of humidity moisten the sleeves of her
blouse.

Will he come?   Or will he not come?   And how
will he be?

I have just finished my sandwich.   Delicious!   A
workman, with a litre of red wine under his arm, passes
quickly along the sidewalk, then dives into a building
where there are other workmen, for this is everybody's
lunch hour.   I am a little giddy looking at the people on
the sidewalk, for I am so close to them that I either see
their heads or their feet.   I find myself looking at the
head and shoulders of a woman, and saying: 'What a
pretty collar!   I must remember exactly how it is cut!'

A moment later my mind notes that in Paris there are still gentlemen with pointed beards who carry stuffed portfolios and examine one in a very penetrating way.

A man has sat down at a table not far from mine. He orders lime tea and tells the waiter that it is because he drank a great deal last night.

'We were a lot of friends together,' he says, raising an arm apologetically. 'This morning, I'm not pleased with myself.'

The waiter smiles as if such confidences are inviolate between men.

'And be so good,' he adds, 'as to send me a shoe-shine boy.'

He glances across at me, and then at the girl in the white blouse, appraising us, but he is obviously too tired to think much about women and his eyes do not linger on either of us, not even on the girl who is so young.

She is by now very agitated.

Solitude does not suit her. Her expression has lost some of its intelligence, and I reflect that if I were a man she would not be the sort of girl I would choose, but in spite of this I am a trifle jealous of her. She powders her face, and taking a very long lipstick paints her lips again, though they certainly do not need it. Her enormous hand-bag is open in front of her. She makes up in public with such dexterity that I watch her fascinated. She passes the comb quickly through her canine coiffure, and puts everything back in the bag. She has a lovely firm bust, but her hands and feet are enormous compared with mine.

The shoe-shine boy has arrived.

He is, of course, Italian. I am not sure about the man's nationality. He speaks to the shoe-shine boy partly in Italian partly in English, but the shoe-shine boy, who is kneeling on two little cushions at the feet of his idol—or of his victim—places cardboard disks between shoe and sock—and then begins the dance of the dusters.

This is the first time I have seen a man's shoes cleaned.

I do not clean mine like this at all. The little Italian dips his fingers in the tin, and then with his finger-tips smears the polish on the shoe so gently, so earnestly, that I am filled with surprise. It is a caress rather than a rub. A delightful smell of beeswax fills the air and now out come three little black brushes, like three little black servants of Regency days, to fly in all directions while the shoe-shine boy says:

'No, sir. I've not been to Naples in thirty years, and I see no reason to go there again before I die.'

A final rub with the velvet rag and the customer, clearly relaxed, is left alone with his lime tea.

I look again at my young friend in the white blouse.

Her blue eyes suddenly light up. Here he is at last! But he is not alone. He is with another girl, a tall blonde, whose hair is done up in a silk kerchief. She looks like a younger Ingrid Bergman.

Ah, but listen to this! My young friend is a German girl!

He puts down a camera and a flashlight, and says in German:

'A salute to the young lady in the white blouse! That would make a good title for a film, *nicht wahr*?'

He introduces the two girls, who smile at each other with ill-disguised animosity, and says:

'She doesn't speak German.'

The trio break into English.

Life has poured back into the features of the girl in the blouse. To think that she struck me a moment ago as less intelligent. Heavens! What a torrent of words, first in German to the man, then in English to the other girl—and now in French!

c

'Yes,' she says with disarming simplicity, 'I learned French during *our* occupation, and I learned English during *their* occupation.'

This explanation staggers me. But is it not merely a question of viewpoint?

They are fashion models. Everything is clear now. He is the photographer. The two girls have suddenly become the best friends in the world and I listen with real interest to an exchange of information about lip-sticks and what one must do not to put on weight. 'I do this . . . I do that . . .' says the German girl, and the mere fact of talking about herself embellishes her. She is prettier than ever. She must be perfectly lovely in a fashion magazine. They suddenly remember they are all hungry:

'Waiter! Waiter! Three roast beef sandwiches and black coffee!'

Now that I am feeling so cool and rested, I would like to walk as far as the rue de Longchamp where, as a little girl, I used to call on my Aunt Marie-Thérèse. Here is the Avenue George V, and the hotel of the same name where I lodged with my son when he was nine years old and a famous film star. We occupied the suite of the Maharajah of Baroda, and all the English colony came to shake us by the hand.

Here is the very modern church of Saint Pierre de Chaillot.

The new building stands on the site of the old one which I knew in my girlhood. My cousin Rolande and I often played in front of it. The architects were wise, I think, to seek their inspiration in the world around them. How foolish to go on building churches in the Gothic style! The great doors are open and I enter timidly, for in spite of my tentative approval, I remain a little shocked. Contemporary sculptors have given Jesus the appearance of an old man, and the Virgin Mary lacks the tender expression and round face of medieval painters. I would have to come here often to feel happy in this church, to rid myself of the curious sensation that I am being introduced to an entirely new religion.

And now where is the rue de Longchamp?

This is the rue de Lubeck with the police-station.

I remember a *gardien de la paix* called Gaston with whom my Uncle Louis often played cards. I thought it very brave of my uncle to call a policeman by his Christian name. There was also a ticket collector on the subway who used to go on duty, clipping tickets, at 8 p.m., which meant that the card games had to end early. When at 10 p.m. we used to go home to Clichy, the ticket collector was in uniform on the platform, and it was he who clipped our tickets. He also raised two fingers to his cap as a salute to my mother and to me, which filled my heart with womanly pride.

Here is the house in the rue de Longchamp.

I look up to where I saw Marie-Thérèse for the last time, her feet resting on a stool, her miserably thin knees pointing up through her skirt, holding in weak fingers the hat she was trimming. She is dead. Rolande, her daughter, is dead. My poor Uncle Louis, also, who was so gay, so good at telling stories, who liked to be surrounded by friends and play cards with them, went to bed all alone one night and, worn out by looking after those he loved, died—the last of the three—in his sleep.

That attic window is the one out of which Rolande and I nearly fell on 2nd August 1914 at the sound of the trumpet call when war was declared. My memory rushes back across the years, and I can see Marie-Thérèse, huddled on a doll's chair, her face hidden in her hands, crying at the thought that Louis, who was pacing up and down beside her, might go.

The windows are closed. Pigeons strut, as they always did, along the zinc gutters.

I would like also to see that other house in the rue de Longchamp, the servants' mews, where, when my aunt and uncle lived there, we gathered every Sunday with the good-looking footman Raoul, the beautiful Hélène, the door-keeper's wife in her long black skirt and cherry-coloured blouse, and poor fat Rose.

The fine block of apartment houses behind which my aunt and uncle lived in their mews flat is still there. I pass without difficulty into the paved courtyard, but though the flats of the rich people remain, the servants' mews have disappeared. There is a temporary door. I open it but it leads to ruins—not the sort of ruins made by bombs but those caused by long neglect. This courtyard, in spite of its charm, gives me the feeling of a cemetery, for here lie buried the memories of my family, my friends, and my girlhood.

I am a little sad, but only a little. I am gently so. I reflect that one day it will be my turn. One always ends by thinking about oneself.

The rue de Longchamp is full of sunshine. Here is the baker's shop where my aunt ordered brown loaves the taste for which she acquired during a trip in England. Marie-Thérèse spent hours gossiping with all these shopkeepers while Rolande and I waited for her. She was such a droll and incorrigible chatterbox. She would say: 'My little girls, I will not be more than twenty minutes!' and we, to forget her absence and our growing hunger, would disguise ourselves in her dresses and pillage her hat-boxes.

Here is the rue du Bouquet de Longchamp, and now I come upon the Avenue Kléber with its magnificent private houses, virtually palaces, with great double doors leading into quiet courtyards. Marie-Thérèse was right, an attic in the heart of Paris is better than an entire

house in a distant suburb. Marie-Thérèse had the
spirit of Paris in her blood. I look for Rolande's school
but I cannot see it. The Galliéra Museum, pretty and
white, which always seemed so large, looks to me like
a wedding cake. The Square des États-Unis, where
President Wilson stayed as the guest of Francis de
Croisset, the playwright, who later became my friend,
is as full of children as it was in my girlhood. There
are prim English nannies also.

The rich children play happily with the poorer ones,
and whereas I wore laced boots in which I pranced like a
young mare, all now have the same little shoes with
crape soles in which they run about silently.

I sit on a bench and am soon joined by a young
woman who has been to fetch a little girl from school.
The child plays awkwardly and laughs stupidly because
of a gaping mouth from which nearly all the teeth are
missing.

'Yes,' says my companion, 'she has been ill. Indeed,
it's a miracle that she is still alive. She must learn to
do each thing all over again. One feels sorry for her
but she improves every day, and it's terribly interesting
for me. There is nothing quite so dull, or quite so
hard, as to look after a perfectly healthy child. My
little one is so gentle, and what is delightful is that she
always needs me.'

As I watch the little girl I notice that as soon as she
has touched a ball or scored a point (for she is playing
hopscotch with two little boys and another girl), she
looks back at her nurse with a pride that quite touches
my heart. The nurse calls to one of the little boys:

'Alain, be a darling and let her win from time to time.'

I learn that Alain is the door-keeper's son, the brightest
and quickest child in the block. Magnanimous, already
aware that boys must be gallant with little girls, he
astutely makes a move that will allow the girl to win.

I am tired. I have walked a long way, but everywhere there are seats under shady trees, and streets and
parks are so beautifully tidy. These republicans are
very proud and careful of what they own.

Regretfully I leave my companion and start to walk
slowly home. A tiny shop in a quiet street attracts me.
There is a sale of brassières. If I could find one I liked,
it would save me going to the big stores, and it amuses
me to buy my lingerie in little shops where things are
often made by hand.

I push the door and go in.

A clean little man in his second half-century stands
behind the counter. His presence in this shop con-
founds me, but I reflect that his wife must be somewhere at the back, and that when I tell him politely that I
want a brassière, he will call her.

But no, he bends down and brings up a tray full of
them. At the touch of his brown fingers, these intimate
things take shape, fill out. Giving me an expert look,
he says:

'This one will suit you perfectly.'

To make even more certain, and before I can resist,
he has encircled my bust with a tape-measure. I lower
my eyes. I blush violently. I am overcome by an
urgent desire to run out of the shop.

What is the matter with me? Am I not a woman who
has borne a child? But what business has a man to sell
brassières? And this curious old gentleman makes me
particularly nervous.

I take out my purse and hurriedly pay for the thing.
As, with relief, I turn to go, he calls after me:

'I have also some very pretty girdles!'

But I scarcely hear him and when, quite flushed, I
reach the end of the picturesque narrow street, I stop
and burst out laughing at my own absurdity.

CHAPTER V

MY TELEPHONE rings, and I hear a young voice:
'This is Ariane Vardon. I am Simone's daughter.'

I search my mind a moment, then give a cry of pleasure.

One evening, during the First World War, when my parents were at supper, our clergyman, who was on leave from the trenches, opened the door. In his beautiful dark blue uniform, with the chaplain's chain and cross, he looked like a crusader returning from the Holy Land. Mme Maroger, his wife, who had creole blood like Napoleon's Josephine, was a lovely woman, and there were three daughters who symbolized my girlish dream of growing up both pretty and clever.

When *The Little Madeleine* was published, one of the first letters I received was from Mme Maroger, and as soon as I was in Paris I wrote to her. Though she planned to remain in the South of France she said that her grand-daughter, Ariane Vardon, would come to see me.

I hurry downstairs, and look round the hall. I am immediately struck by the resemblance of a young woman to the pastor's wife as I remember her in my youth. I introduce myself, and invite her to come up to my apartment to fetch a box of tea I have brought from London for her grandmother. Ariane is tall, a little too strongly built, but what I find really beautiful is her face.

Her complexion is ochre, her eyes are black but the whites have the texture of the very finest porcelain.

The nose is tiny, exquisite, quite captivating.   Cleopatra must have had a nose of this purity of line.   There is not the slightest trace of powder on her face, and she wears no lipstick, and when I cry out in surprise, she answers with delightful simplicity:

'Father dislikes make-up and does not wish me to cut my hair.'

Her big black bun, with the hair tightly drawn away from the forehead, is extremely graceful.   She reminds me of a figure from the Parthenon.   I increasingly rediscover, as I look at her, the entirely natural beauty of Mme Maroger's three daughters who had no make-up to help them.

'I love your hair,' I say, 'but doesn't it worry you to have such pale lips?'

'I haven't a shadow of coquetry,' she answers.   'I never look at myself in a mirror, but I'm perfectly aware that I take after my grandmother who was extremely beautiful.'

Her words amaze me.   I have never met a girl before who says quite calmly: 'I never look at myself in a mirror.   I don't do any of the things that other girls do to make themselves attractive.   I know that I'm beautiful but it leaves me indifferent.'

We are seated side by side, and in the very purest French she talks to me about her family.   Our clergyman, who was so good-looking, died from a heart attack.   There had been the war, lack of money, and two children who came to violent ends, the eldest son burnt to death in a military plane, the youngest daughter, the most brilliant of the girls, a famous young woman barrister, killed in a civilian aeroplane accident.   I am aware of this but I listen to Ariane, dazzled by her beauty.

'Violette's son, Ariel,' she says, 'will certainly make a great name for himself in medicine.   My Uncle Bernard, whom you probably knew as a little boy in shorts, is also a distinguished doctor.'

Ariane continues:

'Mother—you will think of her best as Simone—married a Norman Protestant and is very happy. The only trouble is that I'm not really brilliant at all. I didn't work hard enough at the Sorbonne, and failed in my third year of medicine. I'm doing modern languages now, English mostly.'

My goodness! How serious she is for a young woman of twenty-two!

She reiterates:

'I'm really not good at anything!'

I ask her almost timidly if she is not too grown-up to accept a large tin of English toffee with pictures of the young Queen, Buckingham Palace, and Windsor Castle on the outside. She is delighted, and seeing that the canister of tea also has a coloured portrait of the Queen, exclaims:

'I'll ask granny to give it me when it's empty. Then I shall have two!'

She claps her hands, adding:

'Oh, I am pleased!'

My third-year student is, at heart, only a little girl and I am filled with happiness to have won her heart with such a small gift. We are real friends now and she asks:

'Would you like to come to the Sorbonne?'

'I would love to!'

We rush to the lift, hurry through the dignified hall of the great hotel, jump into a taxi, and cross the Seine. The river shines. The tricolour flies brightly from the Chamber of Deputies. The café terraces on the left bank are animated. It is another glorious day.

The inner courtyard of the Sorbonne is full of young students, swinging their brief-cases against their knees, talking, laughing. One is almost surprised at this sudden contact with so much youth, so many faces in the teen-age groups or early twenties. The contrast with the crowded streets, the café terraces, the busy shops is violent. The people one rubs up against in daily life are graduated like the pearls in a pearl necklace. Each generation is represented. But here I have the curious sensation that all the people about me were born on the same day.

We hurry across to the building marked LITERATURE, as if at the Galeries Lafayette one made for the department marked PERFUMERY. We enter a lecture room where a lecturer is talking about medieval French poetry. Ariane leans over to question a girl in front of us who smiles and shows her note-book. The lecturer is silhouetted against a white sheet. To his left is a blackboard. Several nuns, sitting obliquely because of the narrowness of the benches and the desks, write busily in copy-books, hardly lifting their serious faces. I ask Ariane in a whisper who they are, and she says they are teaching-nuns in convents who follow the lectures at the Sorbonne as refresher courses. I look slowly round the lecture room. We are nearly all women and girls; there are just a few men but one feels that this is feminine territory.

I would love to remain till the end of the lecture, for this is exactly what I enjoy, but Ariane wants to show me other lecture rooms, other buildings.

There are, she says, beautiful panelled lecture rooms hung with superb paintings. We enter one of these and find it three-quarters full. A portrait of Richelieu dominates the scene. Here again we are nearly all of us women. The girls have their hair cut poodle fashion and wear wide tartan skirts. The silence is impressive. One hears only the monotonous drone of the lecturer.

I would like to stay here also. I would like to lose myself amongst all these young women, to identify myself with them, to form with them a single whole, but is it to hear about Richelieu or to become a young woman of twenty again?

I envy desperately their opportunities and their youth. I would willingly give all that I have to start empty-handed again, and yet many of these girls must be terribly afraid of what lies ahead. How few of them will see their dreams come true.

'This is the hardest month of the year,' Ariane whispers to me. 'One must keep on working in spite of the hot weather. There are exams.'

We cross the big courtyard, and a little further along the street we turn into the Medical School.

The scene changes immediately.

Here men predominate. A lecture has just ended and a crowd of youths hurry off on foot, on bicycles, or on Vespas. We go up a flight of stairs to where a lecturer is discoursing on the nervous system. The amphi-theatre is packed with male students, white, black, yellow. As we leave we come up against a most beautiful young man.

'Ah!' exclaims Ariane. 'Here's a friend who is in his third year!'

They face each other, the girl and the boy. Both are incredibly good-looking, but the girl's face, because of the absence of make-up, shows a curious resemblance to the boy's, and as he is tall she no longer seems so massive.

What a splendid pair!

'Well?' he asks. 'How goes it?'

'I failed in my exam,' she says. 'So I'm doing liter-ature. How goes it with you?'

'Fair. It's tough but things are not too bad.'

They shake hands warmly, fraternally, continental fashion.

'What a good-looking boy!' I say to Ariane when he has gone. 'You looked pretty good together.'

She laughs.

'He's charming. His mother is a famous singer. I don't think there is a father. At all events he has never mentioned one to me. Shall we look into the dissection rooms a moment?'

This girl of twenty-two quite dominates me. She says in passing:

'These are the bones. You can buy a bag of them and study them at home. You can't get into trouble with the police. They're painted over with mercurochrome and marked.'

Glass cases exhibit human brains, legs, arms.

'Like it?' asks Ariane.

'It's not so much that I like it,' I answer, 'but it's interesting.'

'Oh, you'll like this much better,' she says, leading me to the dissection rooms. 'It's much more interesting.'

One has to ask permission to go in. Ariane goes over to two men at the door.

'But, of course, my little lady,' one of them answers, laughing. 'Only see to it that you and your girl friend don't take anything away with you!'

What did he mean, not take anything away with us?

The corpses are stretched out on wheeled tables. At first I only see their feet sticking up so very erect. What surprises me is the colour of baked clay that distinguishes them. Because of this unexpected burnt appearance I do not feel any terror. All the same I do not dare look as closely as I would like to. I am afraid of being pursued by horrible nightmares. Some heads are entirely shaved. A student is in the centre of these things, bending over one of them, and suddenly he pulls out a piece of flesh at the end of stout forceps, but this

also is brown. Now, with a look of keen disappointment, he tosses back the piece of flesh into the gaping
aperture. He bends again and with suspended forceps
prepares for another try.

He is all alone amongst these corpses.

'Not too shaken?' asks Ariane.

'Yes, a little.'

'What you see there is nothing. Those things are so
dried up that they are virtually mummies. Come!
It's getting late.'

Little Dutch gardens with flower-beds bordered by
box greet us outside. The gravel crunches under our
heels. Birds fly from branch to branch in cool trees.

'I was wrong to think that I could be a doctor,' says
Ariane suddenly. 'One has to work three times as hard
as a man. They are horrible with us in the exams.
They don't really like us or, to be more exact, they do
their best to discourage us. One needs to have the
sacred flame, if one is a woman, to go through with it.'

The joyous, colourful, noisy streets beckon us, draw
us into their embrace. Medical books that make me
shudder are still on view outside the bookshops, but in
a tiny square, in full view of the Boulevard Saint Germain,
there is a man with two performing monkeys, a large
one and a small one, and all about them is a great assortment of hats, a general's hat, a sailor's hat, a Napoleon
hat, a Tyrolean hat with a feather, and though the
monkeys are almost the same colour as the corpses I
have just been looking at, they are very much alive, and
their antics, as they try on the hats, are so droll that a
huge crowd of students stands in front of them, roaring
with laughter. Ariane and I laugh. We are women
again, gay and irresponsible.

'Let's find a café and talk!' she says.

We talk about Scotland. Scotland is Ariane's passion.
She says:

'I love Scotland and my dream is to marry a Scot.   I spent a wonderful holiday there last year with my girl friend Catriona whom I love.   Life in her house was wonderful.   All the week she wore slacks and her father a kilt, but on Sunday when we went to church, her father wore trousers and Catriona a kilt.   Catriona's father has the ascetic face that appeals to me, the rigid, austere face that I would like to find in the man who marries me.'

As she speaks, I close my eyes and see again the good-looking medical student, and it strikes me that when one is young one is convinced one can choose a husband as one chooses a pretty dress!

We say good-bye.   Ariane will come to fetch me in a few days' time and we shall go to Saint-Cloud to meet her mother Simone, my pastor's daughter, and it strikes me that all these extraordinary mothers and daughters of the Maroger family have a delightful air of a modern *Little Women*.

CHAPTER VI

ON MY RETURN to the Avenue Montaigne, I meet Georges Marin who invites me to join some friends in the bar—Dr Hofmann, a Frenchman who was a fellow prisoner of his at Colditz, Prince Frederick Wilhelm, the Kaiser's grandson ('Little Willie's' son), and the prince's young English wife.

We are introduced. Young Princess Frederick, who was Lady Brigid Guinness, is delightful, intelligent, extremely pretty. I am invited to sit beside her husband, in whose features I find something reminiscent of the Duke of Windsor. He is blond and appears gentle. We drink champagne, and memories come rushing up into my mind. I am somewhat shy and, continuing my thought, say to my neighbour:

'I was a little girl in Paris when you were a very important little German boy.'

He looks at me amused and I wonder what games he played at. Soldiers, I suppose. We become suddenly grown up again and talk politely about theatres, whereupon Lady Brigid tells him that he may find some of the plays in Paris hard to follow because he speaks so little French.

'And yet,' I say to him, 'your father, the Kronprinz, spoke French admirably.'

'That's true,' he answers, 'but I always talk English.'

I feel a little braver and ask him if he was fond of his grandfather.

'Oh yes,' he exclaims, his features becoming animated. 'My grandfather, who was always so severe with his children, was as patient and as gentle as could be with his grandchildren. When I was a very small boy I used to think it wonderful to have an emperor as a grandfather. And it was too, don't you think? When you asked him a question, he always knew the answer.

'In exile he appointed me to represent him at the funeral of King George V, and I was also the guest of King George VI and Queen Elizabeth at their coronation in May 1937. I was still very young. The ceremony was long and intricate, and I was terribly worried because I knew that grandfather would question me closely. I tried desperately to capture every detail, to remember all the names.

'When I found myself in the presence of grandfather, he started off by saying:

'"Now let's imagine the throne is here. The family would have been just there, the peers on this side, the peeresses on that side . . ." And like a field marshal, grouping his armies, he plotted out the ceremony in the Abbey with much greater exactitude than I remembered it. All I could do was to nod assent. "Yes, grandfather, it was just as you say. I remember now. You are quite right, grandfather." He was an extraordinary man. I really did love him!'

He smiles charmingly, and goes on:

'I am very fond of Paris, and I think that grandfather would have liked to be here with me.'

He is not afraid constantly to refer with intimate affection to his grandfather, and I listen to all he says with considerable emotion, for when I was a little girl, did not France and England ring to the call of: 'Hang the Kaiser'? Has a single man ever brought more misery to the world? Now, in the presence of his grandson, hearing him spoken of as a kindly grandfather who would like to be with us in Paris, drinking a glass of champagne, talking about all the things we talk about,

I feel that I have just spent a memorable hour. They rise to go, and he shakes me heartily by the hand, for he has become English in manners and does not employ the continental graces with women. But we smile at each other—the little girl and the little boy who grew up on opposing sides of the Rhine.

I now find myself between the two fellow prisoners of Colditz. Dr Hofmann, young, witty, tender, and enormously interested in the gay, colourful world about him, is a throat, nose, and ear specialist. One has the impression that these men who were severed for so long from the sight and companionship of women, now look upon us as twice-valued flowers in a garden. In their presence I feel even happier than usual to be a woman.

He talks to me about children, poverty, deafness, saying that his immense pity for children occasionally becomes physically unbearable. He adds:

'Normal people—those who see, those who hear, those who have all their faculties—who make such a fuss about a wrinkle or a few ounces of fat, have so many compensating pleasures.'

But he smiles, full of understanding, for he realizes that the search for perfection by women is a cruel, ever-present need, and that it is not in human nature for the misery of the many to stifle the ambition of the few.

He has four children of his own of whom he is passionately fond, and I tell him how, when my son had his tonsils out, and the surgeon showed them to me covered in blood in a jar, I fainted.

'But of course you fainted!' he exclaims. 'I might well have done the same. Only in an emergency could I bring myself to operate on one of my own children. You do not need to be ashamed, madame.'

I tell him how Ariane and I spent the afternoon at the

D

Sorbonne, and how I was struck by the baked clay appearance of the bodies used for dissection.

'You are right to compare them with mummies,' he answers, 'for that is precisely what they are. There is a basement in the building which your girl friend certainly did not show you, where a band of sorcerers (who at home are undoubtedly timid, affectionate husbands) put human bodies sent to them from the hospitals into enormous baths filled with acid, leaving them there for months until they become what you saw this afternoon. After all, these students are not carrying out post-mortems. When I was preparing my thesis, I took a human head home with me. That is my speciality. Others took what they needed. These things are bought by weight.'

'If you wanted a head, you might perhaps have waited until the guillotine had done its work?' I suggest.

'The surgeon under whom I studied had a repugnance to receiving from the State a head without a body, or a fully dressed body, hands tied behind the back, without a head. In this respect he was curiously sensitive. The Germans are sensitive in unexpected ways. The same men who invented the horrors of Belsen punished French peasants for carrying live fowls upside-down, by the legs, to market.'

'Do you remember our cricket at Colditz?' exclaims Georges Marin.

They laugh, eager to tell me the story.

'When things were going badly for them in Russia, the Germans, seeing us rejoice after each disaster, increased their efforts to find secret radio sets. Men equipped with rubber shoes moved noiselessly about, listening. We had a cricket who lived in the potato peelings, and we loved him because of his 'cri-cri.' The Germans mistook our innocent cricket for a radio, and one night the squad, headed by an officer, revolver in hand, broke in. The cricket was too frightened to sing, but in the brutality of the search they killed it, and the officer, holding it between his fingers, realized that the poor little beast had been responsible for the alarm.

'A French officer, whose German was perfect, wrote to the commandant to say that though we were prepared to suffer the rigours of internment, we were shocked that a nation so allegedly chivalrous should declare war on an innocent little beast immortalized by Charles Dickens—the cricket on the hearth. The next day our colleague was summoned into the presence of a German colonel who offered him a cigarette, a glass of brandy, and his most humble apologies for so brutal a murder.'

As we are leaving the bar, Georges Marin says to me:

'Would it amuse you, in your capacity as housewife, to get up at five-thirty to-morrow morning and come with the chef and me to market?'

'Oh yes,' I cry enthusiastically. 'I would love to!'

Five o'clock and it is not yet light, but I am already up.

The french windows are wide open. Paris sleeps as quietly as a village and if, in the streets below, the bakers have already opened their shop doors, no sound floats up to the roof-tops.

If I were energetic I would do physical jerks in front of the open windows, but on second thoughts I will spend half an hour brushing my long hair.

I feel wonderful as I brush my hair rhythmically, with Paris stretched out in front of me. I see myself as the subject of a painting by Toulouse-Lautrec—an attic window, flowers in a pot, slates, and chimney-pots, an ocean of roof-tops, a woman in her petticoat brushing her hair. I have lost all the tiredness I felt in London. I go to the theatre every night, I sup with friends, I go to bed very late, but each morning my body and mind are fresh. I vibrate with the fun of being a woman, of feeling that men realize how important and delightful we are to them.

My coat and skirt are brushed, a white blouse on the chair. I must hurry now. The lift takes me right down to the kitchens. The coffee-maker is waiting for us, and his coffee smells deliciously fresh and fragrant. There are long wooden trays filled with buttery *croissants*, *brioches*, rolls hot from the oven. The chef is here, benign, sipping his coffee, and the coffee-maker offers me a large cup, saying he is sorry there is no saucer. The men habitually drink it like that. A brown carton of French sugar stands open on the table and the pieces of oblong sugar are ranged tightly like dominoes. Already orders from early rising guests echo across the huge kitchens, guests who are catching transcontinental trains or early morning aeroplanes.

The chef leaves us a moment and returns wearing a soft, grey hat which makes him look like an American. Without his tall, white linen chef's hat he seems quite a different person.

'There,' he says gently. 'Finish up your coffee, little lady, we must be going.'

We all thank the coffee-maker and go out into the early morning air where the driver of the light truck shakes hands with each of us. I am put in front, the chef sits at the back.

'What a lovely morning!' he exclaims, and he sounds as if on the point of breaking into song. We reach the Rond Point of the Champs Élysées, and the Place de la Concorde bursts into early morning sunshine. The River Seine shines and looks cool. We drive so fast that I begin to wonder if we are racing against an unseen car. Here is the rue de Rivoli with the gardens of the Tuileries on one side and sleeping shops under arcades on the other. This is the supreme moment of

the day for small cafés that serve white wine to workmen, and bakers' shops that fill the morning air with the
lovely smell of hot bread. A noise, a roar, reaches us
distantly. Our driver does a piece of swift manœuvring,
and we are parked outside the great central markets of
Paris—Les Halles.

Half Paris seems to be congregated in this busy,
noisy, delightful spot. The chef, who tells me that his
name is M. Lucien Diat, has an anxious look, and when
we inquire the reason, he answers very seriously.

'I'm thinking about my tomatoes. Heaven alone
knows what the price will be this morning.'

'Why should tomatoes be expensive this morning?'

'The weather is not quite hot enough for us to get
many from the South of France yet,' says M. Diat.
'Most of them come from Algiers, and there's a shipping
strike. We get a lot of things by air, but oranges and
tomatoes come by sea. So this morning, my little lady,
they will be scarce and expensive.'

'Why don't you take them off the menu?' I ask with
womanly instinct. 'Your guests can perfectly well do
without.'

'No,' answers M. Diat, 'that is not possible. This
is the time of year when a tomato is most agreeable
to the eye. The tomato's glory is during the first hot
days—its presence on the table gives an impression of
coolness.'

We try to keep together but there are incessant cries
of '*Attention!*' as men and women manipulate their
hand-carts on all sides of us. Unlike what one sees at
Covent Garden, the porters of Les Halles carry nothing
on their heads.

'First of all,' says M. Diat, taking us into a narrow
alley, 'I must buy my cheeses.'

We wait patiently while he looks round with an
experienced eye at Camemberts and Pont L'Évêques

from Normandy, and goats' cheeses caked in cinders from the Berry. The goat is apparently very much in favour just now. This patient, solitary, obstinate animal, friend of Greek and Roman shepherd, provides cheeses pyramidal, oblong, and even flat and smooth like certain pebbles on the beach, hard and requiring to be pared with a very sharp knife but delicious indeed with the correct wine. A gruyère from Pontarlier as large as the wheel of a Spanish ox-drawn cart has been spoilt in transit, and a man bargains for it, and takes it away triumphantly on a hand-cart. His face is full of smiles. He will cut it up and sell it quickly at a profit. The cafés are doing tremendous business, and white wine from Burgundy flows from casks.

Here we are at the butchers', for in Paris all the markets are grouped together. These headless carcasses make me quite ill, for my thoughts fly to my own Normandy orchards where my farmer Déliquaire, his sweet wife whose name like mine is Madeleine, and her two sons accompanied by the donkey Jeannette, must at this very moment, as in the fables of La Fontaine, be ambling down our long grassed orchards, under the apple-trees, calling '*teu . . . teu . . .*' to their cows to come and be milked.

Our fish is sold to us by a woman of about sixty, wearing a bright, stylish beret, gold earrings, and a pearl necklace. One feels that she is wealthy and could afford mink. She has an aura of competence rather than of vulgarity. I say something to her, inwardly a little afraid of being laughed at. She has not the quick repartee of the cockney or the New Yorker, and of course she is a person of substance and owns her business. She responds to my inquiry sympathetically, an unseen bond having been established because we are of the same sex. She says:

'I have so many enemies, storms at sea, the trawlers

that don't put out or are so late coming back that they miss the trains, and those chefs who suddenly ask one for two hundred soles of the same size, and then, madame, one is obliged to go through all the boxes looking for the size one wants. I adore my business, madame, but as often as not I don't sleep a wink for worrying There are so many things that can happen to put one out.'

Now we are standing in front of at least a hundred different kinds of sausage from every province of France, some as large as a man's fist, others shrivelled to the hardness of flint—and suddenly I am a little girl again and the date is 1913. My tiny hand is in the huge, rough, tender grasp of my father, Émile Gal, who has talked a great deal in the patois of the Midi to the sellers of smoked hams and sausage-meat who mostly come from his part of the world. There have been tales about the regiment at Nice when he was young, and becoming thirsty he has continued his conversation at the zinc counter of a café, where I sip delicious milk and coffee in a glass and eat hot *croissants* while the men empty numerous little glasses of Chablis. The *croissants* cost one sou each, the milk and coffee have a flavour I have never rediscovered. Time slips gently by and my father has not yet bought the famous smoked ham, to secure which we have got up so early in the morning.

'We have plenty of time, Madelon, for when we have bought our smoked ham we shall have to go home, and it's so good to be here.'

I am seven, and I have made a bouquet of flowers which have fallen on the ground in the flower market and which I have picked up.

The men continue to talk in their rich patois, and soon it will be nine and the market will close. Bells will ring, and men will come with brooms to clean everything up. Here already come the first, very tall, very

strong, with their brooms. The big buyers have done
their business and have gone home, but the little people,
those who count every cent in worn leather purses,
now run from one merchant to the other thinking that
with the bells about to go, they will pick up bargains.
Clang . . . clang . . . clang . . . goes the bell. My father
in his grey cap, sudden understanding lighting up those
bright blue eyes of a true descendant of ancient Gaul,
hurries out, and in a matter of seconds buys our smoked
ham which he drops into a deep sack, to be thrown
picturesquely, fantastically, across his shoulder, as he
strides away with me trotting after him, while passers-
by must wonder if my father is not carrying off in his
sack a dog to drown or some stolen booty.

My mother is not pleased with us. Taking a pencil
from the kitchen drawer and totting up the white wine
drunk with friends from the Midi, the delicious milk
and coffee served to her daughter in a tall glass, the
croissants at one sou each, and the subway tickets—
'No,' says my mother, 'it is not a bargain!' Further-
more, after my father has bought a flask of wine to
bring out the taste of the smoked ham, and sharpened
the carving knife to cut the first slices, well . . . we have
been tricked. The ham is too salted.

'Wait!' says my father. 'Wait till we reach the heart
of it. The heart cannot fail to be delicious. Name of a
pipe! We have only just started to cut it.'

'Fiddlesticks!' says my mother, who, like all her sex,
has not the patience to wait for what she wants.

As I now look again on these narrow streets, on these
old houses, on these cafés, I can almost hear them say:

'We were all here, my little Madeleine, when you
were seven. We saw your father with his blue eyes.
We saw you with your bunch of flowers.'

M. Diat is talking to the sausage merchant. Georges

Marin, who had gone off a moment by himself, now comes back with two enormous bouquets of lilies of the valley, bouquets each of which would make a hundred of those that street vendors sell in the street.

'One for you, Madame Henrey, and one for M. Diat to take back to his wife.'

Oh, what a bouquet! What a beautiful bouquet! Oh, that I could take it to the solitary forgotten grave of my dear poetic father, who when I was seven on this very spot grasped my little hand in his! The sun was as warm as it is to-day. I want desperately to cry. I can merely smile, a smile of thanks for the lilies of the valley whose sweet scent perfumes the air. M. Diat has finished his business. In a few words, without a single gesture, he has bought only the very best and the light truck is already full. I have seen no money exchanged. Rich men do not pay. They are given credit.

'We must be getting back,' says M. Diat.

I shall not see the sweepers with their brooms, nor hear the clanging of the bell. We shall be home long before the market closes.

CHAPTER VII

ON ASCENSION DAY the banks, the insurance companies, the automobile showrooms, the shipping offices—all those vast international organizations that plant marble pillars and vast expanses of plate-glass in the fashionable centres of our European capitals, are closed. I will flee the Champs Élysées and seek the teeming life of the more populated quarters where people, by some miraculous oversight, are still allowed to work and do business on public holidays.

I follow the bank of the Seine in the direction of Notre Dame. There is no sight in the world more beautiful than this. The wide river shaded by magnificent trees, the fishermen casting their lines, the palace of the Louvre that men took six centuries to build, from 1204 till the time of Napoleon, the medieval houses of the Cité, cradle of Paris, surrounded by water—one wonders how it is that friends and enemies, allied politicians especially, have not yet succeeded in destroying so much beauty. Should one kneel on these stones and give thanks to heaven?

I pause for a moment to examine the second-hand books and old prints displayed in boxes under the leafy trees. It is no longer possible to find a bargain here. The world has become too conscious of market values, and there would be swift arbitrage in books on sixteenth-century sorcery or in the poems of lovesick troubadours. Anatole France was the last to find treasures in these boxes, but then he was helped by my cousin Jean Le

Bodo. Books in English are much sought after, for the youth of France, not always conversant with the subtleties of its own language, is encouraged by the State to widen the range of subjects taken at school and university. There is a tiny edition of *She stoops to Conquer*: when I open it I see that it was made in France and bears the translated sub-title: *Elle s'abaisse pour Vaincre*. A handsome white craft, moored to the quayside, flies the Stars and Stripes.

I cross over to the bird market where canaries and love-birds splash colour behind bars. Hundreds of newly hatched chicks make balls of yellow fluff, and when I put a finger in amongst them, they try to peck the red varnish off my nail. The sun is warm, the river gleams, and there are comfortable seats under the trees and café terraces when you are tired. One does not need as in London to tread hot asphalt for ever.

The place to go, when one has searched everywhere else in vain, is the Bazar de l'Hôtel de Ville. This is Everyman's departmental store, the cheapest, the best, the most extraordinary, the warmest, the friendliest, the most colourful, and the most crowded. The management is determined, from the moment you cross the threshold, to win your affection. Music blares at you. Loud-speakers proclaim what is of special interest to buy. The bargains are called out one after the other like the towns and cities on a transcontinental run in a railroad station. 'Have you remembered to buy a white dress for your little girl's first communion?' The first verse of a suitable hymn is broadcast: *Je suis chrétien: Voilà ma gloire!* I am a Christian. This is my glory! 'When you have bought a white dress for your daughter remember, mesdames and mesdemoiselles, that with summer coming along, you should look to the glory of womanhood—a fine, uplifted bust. Brassières, new brassières, glamorous brassières, to make the men notice you. The Bazar de l'Hôtel de Ville thinks of you, ladies, and has your interests at heart.'

Of course it is absurd, but I am impressed. I plunge my hands and arms into mountains of goods piled high on every counter, and I feel amazingly happy. But I must concentrate. I have come here for a specific reason, and the curious thing is that I was advised to do so at one of the most expensive, the most famous, shops in the rue de la Paix.

For some time past I have been looking for a hand-mirror to see comfortably the back of my head when I have rolled up my long hair into a big bun—an old-fashioned oval mirror framed in wood with a wooden handle, like the one the modiste hands you when you go to choose a hat. I am astounded but I cannot find one. I was shown, in the rue de la Paix, plain glass mirrors, mirrors that so magnify one's imperfections that they would give me an inferiority complex for the rest of my life, and other mirrors that I did not want. Then the saleswoman bent down in the friendliest way and whispered:

'Take my tip and go to the Bazar de l'Hôtel de Ville.'

'You think so?'

'Oh, but I know. Between ourselves, madame, I go there every Sunday. They have simply everything.'

I have found my way to the counter but the mirrors displayed in front of me are not exactly what I want. Some are mounted in false ivory which is called 'ivorine,' others in false tortoise-shell called 'écailline,' yet others in plastic glass known as 'plexyglass.' I cannot make the girl understand that I prefer to have my hand-mirror mounted in ordinary wood rather than in these undoubtedly marvellous substitutes whose names she rolls over her tongue with admiration and love.

'Oh, madame,' she implores, 'how can you possibly not simply adore this beautiful plexyglass? It's so

lovely! So transparent! It is I who would appreciate
a mirror like this one! Madame, if I could have just
what I wanted, I would have a whole house built of
plexyglass.'

Well, think I, so the modern girl dreams of the house
of glass we read about in old-fashioned fairy-tales! But
I say to her very gently:

'If I must have something which is false, I think I
will have the false tortoise-shell.'

'Oh!' she says. 'It is pretty, but I prefer this one.'

She takes up the one in plexyglass lovingly and holds
it in front of her. Her twenty years can safely admire
their smooth reflection, but what charms her is that
through the transparent border she can see the world
around her, whereas with the tortoise-shell this attraction
is missing.

Reluctantly she accepts my choice and is about to put
it in a box, when I say:

'Oh, please don't worry about a box. I would
rather you just did it up in paper.'

'No, madame, truly!' she exclaims. 'I could not
allow you to do that. You understand, madame, you
will never leave the store without buying several other
things, and then, suppose you dropped one of your
parcels—you can be quite certain it would be the mirror.
Then, madame, just think of it! Think of breaking a
mirror! I implore you, madame, allow me to put the
mirror in its little box.'

Smiling, she is already beginning to wrap it up in
tissue-paper. I have bought for a few francs the tiny
edition of *She stoops to Conquer* and I ask my pretty little
salesgirl if she will put it in the box with my mirror.
They will be happy together, I think, and this evening
when I open Pandora's Box I shall find Mr Goldsmith's
wit face to face with my reflection. My young friend is
pleased to have made a sale. She gives me the sweetest

smile, and then, like a schoolgirl, licks the point of a pencil and bends over a little book neatly covered with black material in which, I imagine, she is putting down figures.

I leave the store and walk as far as the Lycée Charlemagne whose heavy portal faces the rue de Sévigné, which in turn leads me to the house of this delightful letter-writer with her powdered hair and pannier dress. The house has become a museum, the Carnavalet, a corruption of the name of the original owner, Mme de Kernevenoy, who acquired it in 1578, a house where famous women have lived, and which by all its superimposed images holds one in a fascinated dream, at least if one is a woman and a writer. How many young women writers send me letters from America saying that they have just visited Paris or are about to spend a month here. We seek out, I suspect, the same stones to worship. We are amazingly bound by admiration for those members of our sex who have left great names in that art of letters in which we would so dearly like to shine. There is a curious café with a single table outside, and I sit down at it a moment to breathe the air of the old cobbled street with its flint-grey houses and high windows. I know little about this part of Paris, which makes my adventure more amusing, but I cannot be far from the Boulevard Sebastopol which in my youth was known to apaches and to their girls as the 'Sébasto.'

Losing myself delightfully I now walk without much sense of direction until I come upon a bus stop. A few people are gathered round the post and I ask a woman if the bus she is waiting for goes anywhere near the Place de la Concorde.

'Oh no, madame,' she answers. 'You would do better to walk as far as the Place des Vosges.'

I am about to tell her that I have no idea how to reach

the Place des Vosges when a nun arrives at the head of a long crocodile of little girls. The first half-dozen girls break out of line to ask us if we would like to buy some coloured pictures with saints.

'No, indeed not!' exclaims the woman beside me.

The harshness of her refusal shocks me profoundly, and to make her words sound less cruel to the girls I decide to give them a bright new twenty-franc coin which a few moments earlier I had slipped into the tiny pocket of my tailor-made. These new coins are very pretty.

'There!' I say, offering the coin.

'But a picture costs fifty francs,' says the girl.

'I don't need a picture. I thought you would like the coin for your charity.'

She hesitates, but one of her small companions exclaims:

'What's she take you for? Don't accept her twenty francs!'

'Then give it me back,' I answer, 'but remember that little streams make big rivers.'

The woman whose refusal had shocked me when first the girls asked us for money, puts in:

'You see, madame, that's why I do not help them any more. They either refuse one's charity or take it for granted. Then, on the radio, they tell us small shopkeepers we should not open our shops on Sundays and saints' days. What with the Church and the trade unions, they'll soon have us down to a five-day week like in England. Believe me, madame, to work is as good as to pray. Do they go without their bread on Sundays?'

She pauses, triumphant, and adds:

'If you want the Place des Vosges, it's the second on the left.'

The Place des Vosges is like an exquisite piece of

jewellery, a perfect square, houses with arcades and a most beautiful garden in the centre. Children play on the gravel paths of the garden while grown-ups, seated on iron chairs, gossip as they knit or sew.

Rich and poor live happily together in this delicious retreat. Retired university professors and curators of museums are known especially to favour it. The shops under the arcades include a photographer, a baker, a bookseller of second-hand, rare, and lovely books, and a vendor of knitting-wool. And here is what I was unconsciously looking for—Victor Hugo's house.

From out of this house marched his immense fame, for here it was that he wrote the five-Act play *Hernani*, at whose first performance at the Théâtre Français on a February night in 1830, classics and romantics broke out into an incredible fisticuffs in the course of which, according to Théophile Gautier, aged seventeen, who was there, Mme Émile de Girardin, the most elegant woman writer of her day, golden hair spiralling above her head, applauded the poet for his genius while the audience momentarily stopped fighting to applaud her beauty.

The door-keeper and his wife are sitting behind a barred window. They tell me the house is closed to the public because of the holiday.

'Why don't you both sit in the garden?' I ask. 'It looks so pretty in the sunshine.'

'Oh no,' says the door-keeper. 'We never go there. We sit here and guard the house. Besides, why should we want to go out? It's much more fun to sit here and watch people walk round and round the square. And to-night there is to be a concert in the gardens. We shall be excellently placed.'

A little further on, in a medieval doorway, are two little girls, wide-eyed and dirty. One of them with greedy delight is sucking a shoe-brush, full of black polish, which has already given her a ferocious moustache. I gently point out the dangers of eating shoe-polish but with a cry and a bound she darts, with all the agility of her three years, across the road, from where she makes a grimace at me. A moment later, her curiosity devouring her, she is back at my side. I look at her amazed. She is Cosette, the very spirit of Parisian childhood right out of the pages of *Les Misérables*. The giant's pen is still, but his characters remain.

E

CHAPTER VIII

SUNDAY MORNING, and the weather is less fine. Grey clouds drift above the Paris rooftops, and my balcony is full of sparrows which have taken all this time to discover that I love them. The bells of Saint Pierre de Chaillot have been going since dawn: now they are joined by those of the American church playing a hymn. Last night I listened with some emotion to 'Abide with me.'

I decide against wearing anything too summery. I shall revert to a London-made coat and skirt and a white blouse. I shall look neat if not elegant, and I shall not mind so much if it rains.

M. Jacques, who keeps the very smart news-stand beside the two elevators and the show-cases in which the jewellers of the rue de la Paix show their diamonds, is already arranging the newspapers, magazines, and books of a dozen different countries on his black glass counter. One of the delights of Paris is that while retaining jealously its own history and character, the places frequented by foreigners become immediately international. M. Jacques also sells theatre tickets, and has a name for beating all his colleagues in squeezing two more stalls out of the most popular run in town.

During the occupation, or to be precise, during the early part of it, M. Jacques was known in the 'underground' as Jacques, the friend of Achilles, and his business was to organize the repatriation of allied air crews. This man from Boulogne was captured, tortured, and sent to Buchenwald, and yet he told me one day that his active moments during the war remain his

finest, most treasured memories. I said I supposed
that was the main reason why wars continue to break
out every twenty years: the male mind craves for excitement, will pay any price for it. He said:

'Intense fear, agonizing fear that never leaves one, is
like dope to a man. But also we had power. Here's a
thing, madame, that women find it hard to understand—
how even the most insignificant-looking man, deep
inside him, yearns for power. He gets it to some extent,
in everyday life, at the wheel of a car. The weight and
the speed of the car give him temporary power over
people luckier than himself. He hoots imperiously and
the rich man and the pretty girl run. War gives him
bigger power. When the expected plane from England
came secretly at night, it brought us gold to pay our
agents, paper francs, passports, ration cards, cigarettes,
and chocolate. Our business was to distribute these
things. We gave out tons of money. Though we
were frightened, we enjoyed the power. I organized
human convoys, directing them across France. Now I
arrange—half a dozen novels on my counter.

'I ought not to buy good books. Few people in a
luxury hotel buy good books. They read about murders, pretending that's the clever man's kink. He
must cast off his intelligence when he reads. Is the
intelligence that made him rich enough to stay in this
hotel merely a money intelligence? Has it a blind
spot when it comes to reading? A woman is much
more particular about what she reads, but she has less
money to spend haphazardly than a man.

'English people, who used to set the tone, have other
ideas now. The Americans have rather taken their
place. Here we have many guests from the South
American republics. Their minds work quite dif-
ferently from ours. They will order theatre tickets,
for instance, decide not to go at the last moment, when

it's too late to cancel them, and then be hurt if I ask them to pay. They say: "But as we are not going to the theatre, why do we need to pay for the tickets?" The important thing is not to be angry but to try to explain. They come from countries that still have immense contrasts between poverty and wealth, and when they are very rich, they don't understand why they shouldn't have everything they want.'

I go out into the Avenue Montaigne. The church bells are still ringing. I have a sudden desire to revisit the scenes of my girlhood, to attend morning service at the Protestant church at Clichy of which Ariane's grandfather, Henri Maroger, was the pastor. I can catch a bus opposite Christian Dior which will take me to the Place Clichy, and from there I can follow the avenue till I come to what used to be the city walls of my youth.

The bus is full of men on their way to work, or men taking the children out while their women are presumably working at home. I am the only woman. The children stand on tiptoe between their fathers' legs to see what is going on in the street. We cross the Champs Élysées and climb up to Montmartre.

There is a fair at the Place Clichy and the music of the roundabouts, the loud voices of the show people, and the laughter of the children fill me with delight. I change buses, and this time remain standing on the rear platform which sways up and down like the stern of a ship, while we all lean over the rails and survey both sides of the wide avenue as it slips away behind us. The Avenue de Clichy is long, dirty, and populous. I marvel that as a little girl I was able so quickly to walk from end to end. We reach the city gate where, until the walls were demolished, excise men searched people and vehicles coming in and out of Paris. They lived in a little house whose walls were of glass, and one paid duty on nearly all the goods one took into the proud city. There are no longer any excise men. Their little house and the heavy gates have disappeared. Of the walls themselves, the fortifications as Parisians called them, only occasional traces remain, and gone also are the tram-lines that used to have their terminal at the gates.

The long, yellowed grass at the foot of the city walls was where apaches walked. The capital expanding, breaking the bonds which confined it, has swept away all this picturesqueness. The red neckerchiefed boys with their 'dolls' will now be relegated to story books. One is not quite sure whether to be pleased or sorry.

I jump off the bus and hurry down the street bordered by the cemetery where my mother and I, coming back from Paris, used to meet Mme Gaillard's sister, the road-sweeper, dampening her birch broom with water from the gutter to make a sort of lace fringe on either side of the road. Here is the rue Martre, and—is it possible?—the milk shop, for the milk from whose two or three cows I used to come at dawn when my father was so ill. Now, finally, the rue Gobert, with the small church compressed between two houses which does not appear very changed.

I must be late, for I can hear the sounds of a hymn.

I slip in by a side door which our clergyman and his family used. The church is very full, but seeing a little girl at the end of a row, I ask her in a whisper if I may squeeze myself in beside her, and she says: 'Of course,' and makes room for me.

My young companion listens very sweetly to the rest of the congregation singing, and as I try to remember the words of the hymn, a woman silently leaves her place in an adjoining pew to offer me a hymn book open at the right page, and as we smile at each other, I no longer feel a stranger among humble people in the house of God, among the poor whom Jesus really loved, and I am overwhelmed with love, meekness, and joy, and I sing, I sing with all my soul, for though I have nobody with me, I do not feel alone.

The clergyman sings also, and when the hymn is finished and he climbs into the pulpit there is complete silence.

I have arrived without realizing it on confirmation Sunday. The clergyman reviews the year's progress and announces in a voice full of emotion and thankfulness that through the Grace of God there are several conversions which make him both humble and proud: three girls, two of whom were of the Jewish faith and one of Rome. His features now take on such exultation and joy that one is astounded and moved by the fervour of minority religions.

The girls are the first to go up to him. He calls them by their Christian names. They kneel. He takes their heads between his hands, and says: 'In the name of Jesus, I receive you, my little Jeanne, my little Louise, my little Simone, into the Church,' and one has the impression that these are all members of one large family. The baptism is given with the same simplicity. The 'thou' gives the ceremony something of the Quaker gentleness.

He calls out the number of another hymn, and asks us to be as generous as we can because the church is poor, and it will soon be time to send the small children out of the heat of the city to the seaside, perhaps for a fortnight, possibly longer. That will depend on us.

At the end of the service, we all pass through the vestry where in the days of Pastor Maroger we had our sewing-class. The children who have been confirmed stand in a row, each holding the new Bible which is the

clergyman's gift.   They are surrounded, congratulated,
kissed.   My eyes are damp with tears.   I have prayed fer-
vently.   My mind is full of memories.   Outside the
sun has started to come out.   I go as far as the Place de
la République, past the State school whose trees have
grown immense since I sat for my examination on that
hot summer's day, envying the birds singing in the
branches of those same trees.   What has happened, I
wonder, to my sweet mistress, gentle Mlle Foucher
whose red hair shone like a flaming sun?   And here is
the Gouin Hospital where they cut out my tonsils
without an anaesthetic, and the rue Souchal with the
window at which my mother used to sit, waiting anxiously for my return, and the narrow hall in which, on
the day of his funeral, my father's coffin was placed on
two chairs.   It would be idle to seek his grave.   The
ground is turned over every five years for a new harvest.
Such is the fate of the poor.

Before taking my bus at the Place de la République I
peep down the rue de Mme de Staël.   Her name still
graces it, thank heaven.   No trade unionist, revolutionary, or popular general has yet ousted her as too often
happens to old street names in this part of Clichy.   My
father had his garden down this street, and on the point
of death his thoughts were continually on it, wondering
if the seeds he had planted needed watering.   When my
girlish head was still full of dreams, I had looked up
Mme de Staël in the family dictionary—the Larousse.
'A woman famous for her intelligence and her writing,'
said Larousse.   'Authoress of *Delphine* and *Corinne*,
she paved the way for the romantics.'   The Larousse
had on its title-page the drawing of a young girl blowing
the round seed-head of a dandelion, a dandelion clock
as we used to call them, and the words: '*Je sème à tout
vent.*'   Mme de Staël, my father's garden, and the girl
puffing at the seeds of wisdom all combined at that

time to make me ambitious for the future.　Perhaps the woman famous for her intelligence and her writing blew some of her love of poetry over the gardener's daughter, so that grown up she returns in search of the beginnings that inspired her.

CHAPTER IX

THE NEXT DAY Ariane arrives to take me to her mother's villa at Saint-Cloud. Running lightly across the foyer, she exclaims:

'Am I late? I parked the car at your very doorstep, on the sidewalk under the trees, between two enormous Cadillacs!'

She laughs at her own astuteness. The Cadillac in Paris is not merely the name of one particular make of American automobile. The Cadillac is a symbol of dollar greatness, of well-to-do Paris. There is magic in the name. In the twenties, when we wore short skirts and cloche hats, men talked about their Hispano Suizas. *L'Homme à l'Hispano* was the title of a best-selling novel. The bonnet was tall and long; above the radiator shone the famous silver stork with wings folded downwards. The Hispano symbolized the jazz age on the Continent, the Paris of Maurice Dekobra, Charles Lindbergh, and the *Garçonne*. The Cadillac is the symbol of a new American influence in a Paris as glamorous, as glittering, and as gay in the fifties as it was after an earlier war in the twenties. For though there was a period after the liberation when the French, under Communist influence, thought it fashionable to insult their liberators, they now believe that the American continent represents youth and the future.

I sit beside Ariane in her small car.

She is youth and enthusiasm at the wheel, and we laugh with the joy of living as we race swiftly, expertly, between buses and Vespas, across the Champs Élysées and once again up to Montmartre.

Once again I see the Place Clichy, am borne swiftly along the Avenue de Clichy, but when we reach the gates of the Batignolles cemetery, I put a hand on Ariane's arm and say:

'Oh, Ariane, do let us go and see Paul Verlaine's grave, that wicked fellow who wrote: *Qu'as-tu fait de ta jeunesse?*—What have you done with your youth?'

'Are you sure his grave is in there?' asks Ariane. 'I didn't know. All the same,' she adds, laughing, 'my Scottish girl friend Catriona insisted that I should take her to the Père-Lachaise to see Oscar Wilde's grave, and now you are asking me to visit Paul Verlaine's. It's a strange occupation for the modern woman!'

Just inside the cemetery gates, three keepers wearing dark blue caps with shiny leather peaks are seated on a bench, and one of them is adroitly rolling a cigarette. We ask them to direct us to Verlaine's grave.

'Paul Verlaine . . .' says the one with the cigarette, in a monotonous, guide-book tone without looking up. 'Paul Verlaine. . . .'

He gives us the directions very minutely, and of course we do not understand a word. One of his colleagues puts in:

'Why don't you show these ladies the way? You have plenty of time before your funeral arrives, and as it isn't far we can always watch out for you.'

Still holding the cigarette in both hands, he raises it horizontally to his tongue to moisten the gum, then puts it behind his ear and leads us down a moss-covered path flanked by old and forgotten tombs. The poet's is no better kept than the others, and the name which shines so gloriously in many a bookseller's window is here scarcely readable on the worn stone.

The guide leaves us. He must have wondered what

business we had with the tormented genius whose 1903 edition of *Femmes* bears the notice:

Printed under the cloak, and is nowhere on sale.

Do women read Baudelaire, Rimbaud, and Verlaine, or are these evocative, sensuous, neurotic poems for the most part the cerebral pursuit of men? As a younger woman, such poems shocked me profoundly, and I thought that men who read them must have a vicious streak in their character. I would like to question Ariane about her opinions on Verlaine but I do not dare, and suddenly I realize that while I have been thinking about poetry, Ariane's mind has been occupied with something quite different, for she exclaims:

'Cemeteries are everywhere becoming too small. It's a problem. Where my father comes from in Normandy, the Protestants bought a field in which to bury their dead. A Protestant, in the old days, like a murderer, a highwayman, or a person who committed suicide, had no right to burial among decent people. The graves were often desecrated. So our people bought a field for themselves, but it has become too small. It's a nuisance.'

She looks up—this young girl, so pretty, so gay, so modern, and says:

'Ours is a religion of intelligent people. That's the trouble. Everything about it is simple. One has to be intelligent to understand simple things!'

Her twenty-two years have uttered a solemn declaration of faith, and she is possibly a trifle self-conscious to have spoken so openly, even to me. I marvel. I am full of admiration. What a very serious person is a young woman! What a tremendous, inspiring business being a Protestant in a land where there are so few! That makes it so much more worth fighting for. I look at her fine head cut sharply against the sky, and wish I could follow the rapidly changing thoughts that take place within it.

'I'm terribly happy,' she says as we turn to go.   'I've been invited to spend three weeks at Oxford this summer.'

Now we are back in the car driving through the streets of my girlhood. On Sunday I had seen the State school where I had passed my school certificate: to-day I look eagerly at the Protestant school where Miss Zélie, daughter of a pastor of Montauban, violent-tempered, but excellently brought up, very trim about her person, with pretty waist and boned lace collar—blend of piety and coquetry—had resolutely led her girls forward to a love for God and country. Here is the Boulevard Victor Hugo with the famous public wash-house in which women of all worlds, from the most vulgar to the most respectable, came with their dirty linen. I loved to walk on planks under which the water lapped and gurgled. I can smell again the buttered rolls, *croissants*, hot coffee, and rum that waiters from adjoining cafés sold to the women, while fortune-tellers interpreted the future in the lines of wet palms that smelt agreeably of soap and disinfectant. There are many Arabs in doorways and under trees where in my girlhood we met the apache. Suddenly I recognize the white factory on the Boulevard de la Révolte where the two Dutchmen who made imitation pearls gave me, at the request of Pastor Maroger, my first job, but Ariane is driving her little car so fast that I cannot see whether or not the factory is still busy embellishing our sex. I do not dare ask her to stop, and a few moments later we are in Saint-Cloud.

The villa is enchanting, and as soon as we enter it Ariane calls out very simply to her mother:

'Here we are!'

Simone, the second of the Little Women, comes slowly down the stairs. She wears an orange dress that suits her dark beauty, and I am quite filled with emotion as I see in her the image of her father, the pastor.

She asks me if I remember Mireille, the prettiest and the most brilliant of the three sisters. Mireille and she were at the Lycée Jules Ferry together, and Mireille passed all her examinations with the highest honours that a young woman could obtain, and because she had infinite pity for those in trouble she became a barrister.

'What was extraordinary,' says Simone, 'was to listen to her making a speech for the defence. Her very soul seemed to be bursting out. People rushed in from other parts of the Law Courts. She surprised and held. She had, of course, the eloquence of our father, the Protestant pastor, but in addition she was dazzlingly beautiful. I have never seen, even on the stage, anybody more arresting. The robes, the black toque, and the white bib are extremely becoming to a young and lovely girl. Nothing like her had been seen in the sombre Palais de Justice.

'It is strange to think how many young women dreamed of becoming great barristers. In their new freedom, their equality with men, they thought of it as a prize. There was Portia to fire them. In France there are more young women barristers than in any other country. But even so, how few! One wonders if it was worth all the fuss of the franchise. Mireille was the brilliant exception. The figure that builds a legend.

'She made a wonderful marriage, and lived for a time in Marshal Lyautey's house. His house was curious, dilapidated, picturesque, old, and charming. The famous marshal was always changing his bed from place to place about the house. He could not bear to sleep for long in the same room. The thing became a mania with him. He would give instructions for his bed to be moved to the most strange corners, and he would thus wake up surrounded by the sabres, pistols, swords, rapiers, bayonets, and cutlasses that hung in wild disorder all over his walls. I don't think he cared much what his house looked like or if his constant movings were good for it. He had a nomad mind and had learnt during his soldiering days in Morocco, where his name will live for ever, to sleep anywhere on a hard camp-bed in the desert. The house was so stamped with his personality that even Mireille, who had a tremendous personality of her own, had a hard battle to drive the dead man out of it. She was determined to make the place her own.

'Like all women anxious to shine in a career, she worked twice, if not three, times as hard as a man. That is the price we pay for being women. But in spite of her Protestant side and her legal mind, she was exuberantly gay. The silliest trifle evoked her laughter, and like Ariane here she found time at the height of her work to look after her girl guides. She took pleasure in speed, drove racing cars, and surprised everybody by learning to fly, and obtaining, with no apparent effort, her pilot's licence. When her husband asked her where she would like to go for their honeymoon she chose the penal settlement of Devil's Island, off the coast of French Guiana, of which she had heard so much in the Law Courts, and on her return she wrote a book that shook the country and led to the abolition of that romantic but pestilential prison.

'She adored travelling and was a delightful person to travel with. One followed in her steps, one not merely listened to but also looked at her when she spoke. With me she was gay, learned, and facetious. She used to make little paper boats that she left lying about everywhere, and that I would discover in the bath-room, on the soap, in front of my looking-glass; and she used to tell me that she had put them there to amuse me and so that I should know she was thinking of me.

'I wonder if the combination of a lovely girl and exceptional brains is not too much for a mortal. Beauty and wealth, yes. Beauty and great position, yes. But beauty and brains . . . those make a formidable combination.

'Amazing things happened to her.

'Clasping in both hands a magnificent bouquet of red roses which somebody sent her, she pricked a finger, and instead of going to sleep for a hundred years like the Sleeping Princess, she developed septicaemia from which she nearly died.

'When she was convalescing, she asked me to come with her to Morocco. Then it was that the aeroplane in which we were travelling crashed. Mireille was only twenty-seven. She was killed outright. I think she had never looked more beautiful. Her fame was already great. She was the rose plucked in all its magnificence.'

'And you?' I ask.

'Oh, I,' says Simone, 'I was merely among the injured.'

We talk about the days when my mother and I lived in Clichy, taking up a name here, another there, gathering up quickly in the first excitement of our reunion the great gallery of picturesque characters which peopled our youth.

'There was Mme Maurer . . . you remember Mme Maurer to whom I went so often to borrow a book, she who instilled in me the taste for reading? Her father had been a great actor at the Imperial Theatre, and Napoleon III had given him a medal. You know that Mme Maurer died?' I say.

'I do,' answers Simone, 'and towards the last when she was bedridden, making artificial flowers all alone at the very top of the house, a woman called Mme Pocho looked after her. Mme Pocho had the most beautiful blue eyes and the head of a doll, and out of compassion would send a plate of hot stew from her own pot to Mme Maurer. She would also go to make her bed in the morning, but she was always so terrified of finding Mme Maurer dead, that she implored her never to close her door. Mme Maurer, poor soul, had no objection. She owned nothing but a transparent globe under which she kept what she called her relics—an alabaster vase, and the medal Napoleon III gave her father. It was for some play in which the great actor had played the role of Napoleon I. Mme Pocho also came to tidy the rectory. When my father retired, Mme Pocho worked for me. She had three little children, and was about to have a fourth when she had a miscarriage and died.

'Then there was the family Boucry. I must tell you about them.

'Mme Boucry had eleven children of whom Germaine —you knew her—became a dancer at the Châtelet where they give all the big musicals in Paris, charmed the capital by her beauty, and married an authentic French nobleman. There was Berthe who married a Spaniard who carried her off to Spain, but at the height of her beauty she was killed in street fighting during the civil war. Henriette, the youngest girl, is with her mother who lives at Marrakesh in Morocco where she owns an important bakery.

'So you see that the girls of Clichy have done rather well in the world—my sister Mireille, the dancer of the Châtelet, and yourself, my little Madeleine.'

The pastor of Saint-Cloud is announced.

Dressed in a brown corduroy jacket, his neat person reminds me of my friend, Maître Vincent, my notary. He asks Simone for news of her husband who is ill, and then turns to various parochial problems. I gather that though his parish of Saint-Cloud is not by any means a poor one, he has much on his mind. He is in search of young women to lead the girl guides and the very small scouts, and he tells Ariane that although he wants to send as many children as he can to the country this summer, he is worried about the attitude of the children themselves.

'They no longer have any respect for what belongs to others,' he says, 'and not the smallest notion of gratitude. If you lend them a country house or an orchard, you mustn't expect any thanks, only smashed window panes and broken fences. And if, in spite of this, you want to be charitable, you must be content with your own good deed—for the children and their parents will merely claim that they have a right not only to what you have given them, but to more besides. Do not imagine, for instance, that when you have lodged them, fed them, and amused them for three weeks, they will come to serenade you, recite a little poem of thanks, sing a hymn, or present you with a bouquet of wild flowers.'

'Yet,' says Simone, 'we do not give up. The road is merely a little harder. One needs a bit more courage, and the rare thanks we are given tastes all the sweeter.'

'Of course,' answers the pastor, 'and our efforts to give children three weeks at the seaside must be the great thing with us. It is, however, most unjust that the parents who are given money by the State for their children's holiday, keep it for their own pleasures, and we are very lucky if they will even entrust their children to our care.'

Ariane mentions a young woman in whom she has much faith. The pastor is not so certain she will make a good leader for the girl guides, not that he has any doubts about her, but he says:

F

'The trouble about our young women is that there are so few Protestants for them to marry. Love does not any longer take religion into account. Of course, whether they are Protestant or Roman Catholic they should put the love of Jesus first, but I fear that what generally happens is that after marriage they just cease to be one thing or the other. It would be almost better for them to have a good fight about their respective religions than to settle down comfortably into an existence of television and unbelief. There is something so cold and cynical about it. The devil is the winner and the children will grow up to worship the State.'

Ariane and I feel that the conversation is becoming a little deep for us, and we leave the pastor of Saint-Cloud to Simone. Ariane says she wants to drive me back to Paris.

This time we follow the banks of the Seine, for I would like to find the villa along the towing-path where as a little girl during the First World War I stayed with Lucie, the lodge-keeper. I remember a belvedere and barges along a muddy bank, the oilcloth designed with a pack of playing-cards on which we ate our meals (each of us girls and women fighting to have the jack of hearts), armfuls of lilac, delightful games of hide and seek in the woods, and the sudden sight of soldiers bivouacking.

I search diligently but I cannot find the villa. Everything is changed and there are a great many petrol pumps.

Ariane has become herself a little girl. She breaks out into glorious laughter. She drives her car as if it were a scooter in a fun fair, argues, gesticulates, gives the impression of wanting to come to blows with young men driving immense trucks who bend out of their cabs to insult, then seeing so young and pretty a girl, change over to laughter and pretty compliments. We go at full speed down wrong streets, put ourselves skilfully into reverse, and start off again joyfully in the right direction. We bounce over cobble-stones like sisters rushing to the ball in a pumpkin. Ariane's happiness is contagious. I would go thus with her to the end of the world. Statues of generals and frock-coated politicians which dot the streets seem to fly at our approach. We return gloriously to the heart of Paris.

I have time before dinner to fetch my dress from the cleaners.

I look forward very much to having it back again, for I remember how sweetly the woman said to me:

'Madame, your dress will be so pretty when we have finished with it! I will iron it carefully, and you will be proud to wear it.'

So off I go to the street of that divine love poet, Clément Marot, and to the cleaners. This time there are two women behind the counter, the one who took my dress in, and another, both not very young spinsters. They say they are very sorry, but because of the many national holidays during the past ten days, the factory has been more often closed than open, and my dress is not yet ready.

I look at them with suspicion. I am not pleased. I think they are both very ugly, even older than I thought, and their hair is unevenly dyed. I try to give some forcible expression to my displeasure.

'What do you want us to do about it, madame? Do you suppose that we are in a position to argue with the shop-stewards in the factory? I would like you to go and see for yourself, madame. They open their factory and they close it just as they please. They don't care a pin about customers like you. And it's because of them, the people in the factory, that *we* poor elderly women must go on working behind this counter. The price of living goes up because of *them*, because of the money they want for the hours they *don't* work, and instead of spinsters like my colleague and me being able to retire to a little house just outside Paris which our parents spent all their lives buying for us—we, madame, must go on, we must continue to take in dresses and argue with our customers, instead of sitting quietly in the shade of our garden. Yet, madame, see how cruel life is to lonely women who grow old. The young people at the factory are not pleased because we go on working, my colleague and I. They say we are too old, that we prevent younger people from having our jobs. But do you suppose that it amuses us, madame, to stay here all day behind the counter, and when we go out to walk on the hard asphalt instead of admiring the green lawns and roses in our garden? Let them grow old themselves! To think that all my savings have gone in devaluations and every other kind of State thieving, just to pay their welfare schemes!'

Before this unexpected speech I stand abashed, perplexed. They are two against one, and I am a little frightened of them. I reply that I regret having asked somewhat abruptly for my dress and that, of course, I can do perfectly well without it for another two or three days. I feel ashamed, as I always do on these occasions, to realize suddenly how lucky I am compared with so many other women. I am almost blushing as I leave their shop.

I go next door to the newsagent who also sells ribbons and hairpins, and I ask for my woman's fashion paper. The old lady scurries from the haberdashery counter to the magazine counter and says:

'Madame, your paper hasn't come out this week. I

don't know whether it's the holidays or if they are on strike.'

I feel rather uncomfortable as if it were all my fault, but I feel happy also because it is such a lovely evening, and though I have now worn them for ten days I am still deliriously pleased with the very high heels of my new shoes.

My Greek shoemaker is standing in front of his shop.

He is wearing an apron and his shirt-sleeves are rolled up above his elbows.   A vast smile lightens his face.

'I love my shoes,' I say, 'but they hurt a little.'

'Of course,' he exclaims.   'Little madame not heard thunder in the night?   Another storm, perhaps, to-night.   Is little madame still much in love with idea of having red shoes?'

'You said that red shoes were not worn much in Paris because women here are too practical.'

'But if THOU likest red shoes, little madame?   Always buy what the heart desires.   Especially if money can satisfy thy desires.   I would buy . . .'

He stops a moment, thinks, looks up into the evening sky and continues:

'I do not truly know what I would buy.'

'Perhaps you are entirely happy in your little narrow shop, between one shoe and another?   Perhaps you have no desires?'

But he has made me think of those red shoes again. I shall never be reasonable.

Two American women pass along the street.   They look into the shoemaker's window, and as they continue their way one says to the other:

'I don't like those shoes.'

'Please, little madame, tell me what American ladies said?'

'They said your shoes were very beautiful.'

'Perhaps they say so,' says the shoemaker, 'but there was no love in their eyes, and I know when women have love in their hearts or in their heads.   Love even for a pair of shoes is quite easy to see.   I can even tell it by looking at their feet.   Love shows itself everywhere. Thus ladies sometimes come to my shop after long absence.   They say: "We want many shoes, many." And they dance on their pretty feet.   Then, little madame, I know they are in love. Thou understandeth?'

CHAPTER X

THAT PART of Paris round the Bourse—the Stock Exchange—is very gay. I arrive by the rue du 4 Septembre. A young woman in a lottery booth, lottery tickets all round her, is in the middle of a very animated conversation which I have the temerity to break into.

'Mademoiselle, would you be very kind, and direct me to the General Post Office?'

She looks up surprised to be asked such a silly question, and not at all pleased to have the flow of her conversation interrupted, and she hurls her answer at me as if I were expected to catch it like a ball in mid air.

'Behind the Bourse, madame.'

That is precisely what the porter at the Plaza-Athénée had told me, but I am still very stupid at finding my way about, and my lack of comprehension shows on my face. The young woman in the lottery booth, annoyed that I should stand there, preventing her from getting on with whatever she was explaining so volubly, repeats in a louder, shriller voice:

'Behind the Bourse, *madame*. What more do you want?'

It is midday, and everywhere I look I see charming restaurants with gay terraces at which people are lunching in the open air. The Stock Exchange, temple of High Finance, built like a Roman temple, stands here with its wide steps and pillars, so noisy with the clamour of countless voices that one has the impression that a revolution has begun. I climb the many steps and am

79

about to seek an entry, when a *sergent de ville* lifts his blue cape to bar my way and says:

'Come, madame, don't you know that women are not allowed in here? If you had put on trousers, I might not have noticed you from a distance, but'—he turns his twinkling eyes with a show of great delight on the inescapable roundness shaping my blouse and the front of my jacket—'I think, madame, you will admit that I am well and truly in the presence of a woman trying to make her way into the Bourse.'

I blush and laugh at the same time.

Only a Parisian policeman could compose so rapid and elegant a speech to soften the implementation of the law. What fun it is being a woman in Paris!

'I am terribly sorry,' I answer. 'I thought perhaps one was allowed to peep in. As a matter of fact I am looking for the General Post Office.'

This is indeed a sumptuous post office.

The French post offices after being the most sordid are now the prettiest on the Continent. The large and important ones are marble palaces, and the pretty girl who takes my envelope, her hair dressed in the inevitable poodle fashion, looks as if she is in a glass case. This girl is more than pretty. I can hardly believe the scene in front of me is not out of the Folies Bergères, and that the girl is not a famous star. With her dolls' scales beside her, I fully expect her to break into song. She weighs my letter, finds suitable stamps in a linen-covered book, tears them out, and gives them to me with my envelope. But she looks so terribly bored that her beauty is frigid, like the glass in which her tiny figure and the shining metal scales are encased. It is all so beautiful that it ceases to have a soul.

As I emerge into the sunlight, a young woman asks me to direct her to the rue Vivienne. I suddenly remember that she was sitting beside me in the bus that I boarded at the Rond Point. As I am myself going to look for this very street, we decide to seek it out together. She is very slim. I doubt if she has more than a twenty-two-inch waist, and I had been very surprised in the bus when she suddenly showed the conductor a pass accorded to mothers of large families.

'Yes,' she says, 'I already have five children, two of them twins. A friend has given me the address of a wholesale house in the rue Vivienne where I thought I might get some cheap prints to make up into dresses for the summer holidays.'

The rue Vivienne is long, and I only know half of it.

When my mother and I came to Paris so that I should learn hairdressing, we crossed by Newhaven–Dieppe and arrived at the Gare Saint-Lazare just before five in the morning. We had been given the name of a tiny hotel between the vegetable market and the Bourse, where for sixteen francs we could have an attic with a clean bed and running water. Leaving my mother in the taxi, I ran up several flights of private flats to the top of the building where, at the end of a corridor, I found a glass door with some keys hanging from a board. A woman, having thrown a dressing-gown over her night-dress, asked me what I meant by waking her so early, but noticing my youth and confusion she gave me a key which I hurriedly took down to my mother.

I find that this house still exists, and I come across the rue des Petits Champs down which I used to go every morning to my hairdressing school in the rue de Rivoli.

There is a small café with a zinc bar and some tables set for lunch against a wall. I am hungry. This is the place for me. I shall be able to see everything going on both inside the café and outside in the crowded, narrow street.

I do not have long to wait. A young woman comes

to the bar and asks for a sandwich, for she is going to the hairdresser and will not have time to lunch. The owner of the café goes to a table, cuts a long piece of French bread, slices it lengthways, butters it, fills it with ham, wraps it in paper, and gives it to the young woman who hurries off on her very high heels.

Two men seated at the short zinc bar are lunching with a bottle of red wine between them. A man of about thirty whose blond beard gives him an old-fashioned appearance arrives with a mastiff, and also goes to the bar where he calls for a steak and fried potatoes and a dish of raw meat for his 'little' dog. He smiles in a friendly way at the serving girl, and asks:

'Why didn't you answer when I knocked on your door last night? My car was full of peonies. I brought masses for the *patronne* and for you. Had you gone out?'

'No, I was there,' she says. 'If I had guessed you were bringing me flowers, I would have opened the door. Did you give them all to the *patronne*?'

'Of course! What should I do with a lot of peonies in my room?'

Suddenly I become aware that the whole place is full of red, white, and pink peonies. They are truly lovely.

When the bearded man's steak arrives the *patronne*, who is extremely young, appears and says she cannot make out why his parents have peonies already in bloom whereas those in her garden are still in bud.

'I think your parents must be sorcerers!' she exclaims, laughing.

'No,' he answers, quite seriously. 'Just ordinary, honest people, but they protect their peonies from cold winds. They look after them like children. I can assure you they don't do as much for me!'

He adds good-humouredly:

'They like my dog, though. They say he's better behaved in a garden than most modern children.'

The conversation continues about peonies until the end of lunch. What shall I do this afternoon? The weather is not quite so sunny, and the peonies and the red wine have gone a little to my head. I shall begin by walking along these narrow streets filled with memories of Richelieu and Louis XIII as far as the Théâtre Français.

I am amazed when I walk alone through the streets of a city how the hours give a full measure of strange happenings, unexpected treasures. No care comes suddenly to disturb my thoughts as I look into a shop window or watch some artisan at work, a laundress ironing skilfully, a girl sewing; and for the first time since my girlhood I enjoy the incomparable fun of the street scene.

In the Avenue de l'Opéra a bus comes to a halt beside me, and I am so struck by this invitation that I jump into it and book to the terminus. When the conductor discovers that I do not know where he is going he laughs at me, but a woman sitting opposite takes my side and cries:

'And why shouldn't the lady go to the end of your route? Do you suppose it's uninhabited?'

We cross the boulevards, skirt the Galeries Lafayette, and start climbing towards Montmartre. I am enchanted. As we pass the famous closed cemetery of Montmartre, the first page of the younger Dumas' *La Dame aux Camélias* springs open. Armand Duval, who has brought misery upon two hearts by obeying his father, now wants to see his beloved who is dead. Perhaps there is something in the modern French idea that one should satisfy all one's desires, brooking no interference. Literature is full of tragedies brought about by filial obedience. Who would not murder Oswald for not making up his mind to marry Corinne? Certainly there is an influence in the Paris of to-day that one begins to feel before one has lived there very long. The complete absence of hypocrisy in the domain of love is so apparent that one continually sees young people kissing each other passionately, and old people affectionately embracing one another without fear of ridicule. I who explore Paris alone see these things and am warmed by them.

We pass tiny, old-fashioned shops that give one a delicious idea that they have come out of a fairy-tale. The people inside them, I feel certain, remain as violently individualistic as the goods they sell differ from those in the shop next door. Everywhere also in this agglomeration of villages that makes a big city are gay cafés with tables and chairs outside, trees spreading cool, green boughs, and little squares no larger than a handkerchief in which children play.

The bus stops outside the Bretonneau Hospital where my baby brother died. If I had known that it was the memory of my little brother that was waiting for me at the end of this bus ride which I had counted on being so joyful, I would not have come. In an instant, I see my mother all in black, during that bad winter in 1912 when she had just lost her baby son. I cry, not precisely for him. She is probably the one to cry over. I have the impression that little pieces of my girlhood remain caught up like shreds of a torn dress in all the streets of Paris. I see things too vividly, though often my mind slips back into periods sealed off one from the other. Is it an advantage or quite the reverse to be gifted with an astounding memory? Simone said to me in her villa at Saint-Cloud: 'We cannot understand how you remembered so many things!' I told her that not having been to school, in the true sense of the word, as a little girl, and my mind, in consequence, not having been cluttered up with too much injected knowledge, my eyes, my ears, and my heart—yes,

especially my heart—had been left wide open to the
world about me. My university was the street. And
now it would appear that I was going back to the street
for a refresher course!

I take another bus which brings me to the foot of
Montmartre where a woman with a child says to me:

'If you take the rue des Saules, madame, you will be
at the top in no time, and it's really nice up there when
the sun comes out. My little boy and I are just back
from Beaujon where we have been to visit his father
who fell off a ladder on a building job, so that he is now
in hospital for three months. Of course, with the
national insurance and all the rest, I don't need to worry
so much about the money, but it's hard luck, isn't it?
He's my second husband. I married first at eighteen
and was a widow at nineteen. Now I have two
other children besides this one and a nice apartment
opposite.'

I climb the rue des Saules, and reach the corner of the
rue Ravignan and the rue Norvins, and at the sight of a
baker's shop I suddenly recall that it was here that my
son, after his triumphal first night, marched at the
head of the Poulbot children with drum and fife band
through the cobbled streets.

Poulbot's name was immortalized by his drawings of
the children of Montmartre whom he sketched when I
was a little girl, so that I might well have been caught
by his pen. He passionately loved his wife, Montmartre, and the children of the street, for whom he left
money. Because I had been a girl here, the film people
arranged for my son to attend an open-air tea-party at
which girls and boys, dressed in Napoleonic uniform
with the sansculotte bonnet, entertained him. One of
the little *cantinières* (the girls who followed armies with
food and drink), with a small cask tied to her hip,
offered me a lovely bunch of flowers—and I kissed her

in the glare of the arc-lamps. It was charming—and already so long ago!

Here is the Place du Tertre crowded with artists who sit under the trees whose leafy boughs touch one another. Though Montmartre is always full of foreigners, it remains essentially itself, extremely French, smelling of garlic and oil—and the people one sees looking out of the windows, or going with their baskets to market, could not be more native to the soil. They live here, they breathe the clear air, and accept in good part the foreign tourists.

Benediction is in progress at the Sacré-Cœur, and there I find a good many women, a few men, but practically no young people. Incense perfumes the basilica, and a woman beside me kisses with simple devotion a number of holy pictures which she brings out of a prayer book.

The high altar is impressive, and the priest in his brocade vestment appears to be without feet. His cope is beautiful and wide: his person small in stature. The choristers have pretty, pink faces, but their hair stands up like the bristles of a brush. A tricolour flag fringed with gold and the white standard of Jeanne d'Arc hang above them.

A coach has arrived and tourists begin to file into the service, which obliges me to move slowly against the wall, where I find myself inspecting a large coloured photograph of a Touareg, member of that fierce nomad tribe in the Sahara, and I read that an exhibition in honour of Father Charles de Foucauld is being held in the crypt.

This brilliant officer of the cavalry school of Saumur lived too gaily in the days when titles and wealth meant so much. Still young, he decided to expiate his excesses by a change of heart. He became a priest, went to North Africa, and before being murdered played a role as colourful as that of Marshal Lyautey himself.

I look with curiosity at several exhibits—the altar he made in the desert so that he could hold his first mass, the cross fashioned in this ocean of sand where there was no wood, the communion cup, and the tabernacle.

'I have just been ordained,' he said, 'and I want to follow in the steps of Jesus, not to preach, but to live in solitude, poverty, and the humble work of our Saviour.'

On tablets the size of a postcard, he carved the Stations of the Cross, marvels of simplicity, and here we have his hatchet, hammer, and saw. He said:

'When one goes away saying that one is going to do something, one must not return without having accomplished it.'

He founded the order of the Little Brothers and desired that everybody, Christians, Jews, Mohammedans, and heathens, should regard him as a brother. To Lyautey, in his work of pacification, Charles de Foucauld was doubtless a magnificent aid, and though it is now fashionable to decry the builders of our respective colonial empires, one may suppose that these men were at least as good and just as those who have allowed them to crumble.

Little Sisters, of whom there is an order also in North Africa, come to see these relics of Little Brother. There is a photograph of one Little Sister, as black as night, tenderly caring for a leper.

An aged priest is selling booklets, and because he is not accustomed to handling money, he counts his change like a small child, saying:

'A mistake would be as serious on one side as on the other. I must not rob the kind friends who buy my little books, but the missions are so very much in need of money. So I have to be very careful.'

Under his skull-cap in the yellow light of the crypt,

he looks like the wax figures of Little Brothers that are dotted realistically about.   Only the fact that he counts his money so anxiously reassures me.

I am enchanted by my pilgrimage to the Sacré-Cœur, and I feel quite serene as, returning to the Place du Tertre, I see the restaurant of the Mère Catherine, where so many famous painters gathered in the days of their poverty.   In Montmartre one can both pray and laugh. The Montmartre is the name of the vine, already forming tiny grapes, that grows sturdily on a miniature hillside protected behind by a stone wall covered with wistaria, irises, and carnations.   Poets and painters who achieved celebrity before their death are buried in the little cemetery of Saint-Vincent.   Those who died poor and miserable like Modogliani, were taken to Saint-Ouen for a pauper's funeral.   Two workmen seated on a tombstone are talking in a mixture of French and Italian as they take turns at a bottle of red wine. For the tall, narrow houses round, with their French-looking windows, this quiet spot is in effect a garden, for the gates are closed in the evening and all becomes countrified.

As I am on the point of leaving, I notice that the tenants of a first-floor window have let down two porridge pots on the grass by long strings.   One contains some elegantly chopped raw meat; the other fresh cream.   A cat, who does not mind my presence in the least, goes from one pot to the other, eating her meat delicately, lapping her cream, turning from time to time to purr at me.

I suppose that when Mme Miaow has finished her dinner, she will go proudly away, and the tenants of the first-floor window will draw up their empty pots.

CHAPTER XI

MAGIC, like Puck running along the telephone wires, enters my home on the roof-tops.

The telephone, which in Paris only a short time ago was rather a haphazard thing, has now made startling progress. Mine, for instance, which looks very elegant by the side of my bed, has been ringing all the morning. The lady who has the room next to mine also has a telephone, and she has not ceased to talk into it.

She and I became aware from the very first that, because of our wide-open balconies and shrill feminine voices, each could hear every word of what the other said. We decided, by telepathic modesty, to modulate our speaking tones, but after the first word or two of each conversation, carried away by excitement, we throw caution right over the chimney-pots and let ourselves go into a full-throated, happy, and completely natural soprano.

One of the advantages of living alone is that one can start work very early in the morning. Before seven I have telephoned for breakfast, and I am quite amazed at the succession of extremely handsome young men who at this very early hour wheel in the coffee, milk, and hot rolls. They are not only young, which in itself is a breath of spring, but impeccably dressed in white jackets which are freshly laundered and as warm from the iron as the bread and *croissants* are hot from the bakery. The French, like the Americans, are right to dress young people in a young way, and not ask waiters at 7 a.m. to appear in black tail suits and false shirt-fronts that presumably date from stage-coach coffee-houses in Napoleonic times.

I throw a little bread to the birds.

The Eiffel Tower, which revolves its beams until far into the night, its waist garlanded with coloured lamps, has its summit capped this morning in white cloud. The base stands vigorously against the curling smoke of a waking city.

Normally the lady next door sleeps till nine-thirty. Without knowing her, without even having set eyes on her, I am acutely aware of her presence, and I feel that our nearness to one another is a bond between us.

This morning, even before eight, she has seized the telephone and is asking for the *concierge*. She speaks French perfectly but with a slight American accent, perhaps even with a slight Russian one also, that is typical of a foreigner who lives for lengthy periods in Paris and accordingly forms part of the cosmopolitan society of the city. One hears this accent when one tries a dress on in one of the big dressmaking houses, at Dior or Balmain, for instance, and one is almost tempted to adopt it as one adopts the international cuisine of the big hotel or the ocean liner. I find it delicate, delicious, at times urbane, at other times acidulated as if evoking the steppes (before the Iron Curtain cut them off), the Rocky Mountains, Boston, Mexico City, or Rio, and evocative of the women who have in common their love of Paris because they find here the right atmosphere in which to laugh, to dance, to love, to dress, and to gossip.

The head porter is downstairs listening very attentively. Exquisitely, for she is a woman of impor-tance, with much knowledge of the world, she tells him that she has lost a very fine gold box, mislaid perhaps in a taxi, and if by any chance it were to be brought back to the hotel, would the head porter have the great kindness to advise her immediately . . . and so on.

After this we make a tour of all the mansions and the apartments where she visited friends the previous day. She asks, in each case, to be put through to the personal maid:

'. . . No, please, I insist, do not wake up madame, but I would like you, my dear Marie, to be very, very kind and pass your hand behind the cushions of the arm-chairs and settees in which I might possibly have sat yesterday, and see if you cannot find a gold box I have lost. You will? That is really very sweet of you, my dear Marie, and you will ring me back, won't you?'

My own telephone rings.

I am invited to a children's party in a large private house just off the Champs Élysées. Mostly little girls? Yes, I would love to come. Punctually at four? Thank you very much.

I put down the receiver. The telephone rings in my neighbour's room.

'Oh, my darling, so your maid has already told you? I had given her the strictest orders not to wake you up, but how extremely kind of you to want to talk to me! So now you know the terrible news—my beautiful box, the very exquisite one in three different colours of gold made by Fabergé, a real museum piece! I really love it, and I always carried it about with me. But, my darling, it was so very heavy, I would have surely heard it fall! How can I thank you sufficiently for asking your servants to turn your beautiful house upside-down to look for it, but I might have guessed that you would understand my worry and grief. It just happens to be a thing I love particularly. I have lost so much, been robbed so often, but always carried the box in my hand-bag. Truly, my darling, I am a most unhappy woman. Everything is going wrong just now. A whole lot of worries at the same time. You say that Marie has looked everywhere and cannot find it? Well, my darling, thank you all the same. I shall have to persevere.'

She has hardly put down the receiver when her telephone rings again. Her masseur is asking for instructions, and as a woman tells everything to her masseur, she immediately recounts her loss, but as he is in the habit of going to her, and not she to him, the poor man will not be able to elucidate the mystery.

Now she rings another friend.

'Ah, there you are, my darling. Listen! I must tell you that yesterday I lost my gold box, yes, exactly —the one you always so greatly admired. No, alas, I did not come to you yesterday. I should really be telling you about the night before last. A real success. A charming evening. Everybody was there, Mrs X with young Z and one or two extremely pretty dresses. And do you know who that boy was who danced all the evening with the little T girl? Ah! So you know about it already! I understand that it's been going on for the last fortnight, and I only discovered about it at the party. I was made to feel quite silly. When I see you this evening I must tell you what my lawyer says. I am going to see him at midday. Yes, isn't it a bore? Well, good-bye, darling. Oh, I was forgetting to tell you that little G hadn't yet had her baby when I left New York on Saturday. Good-bye, my darling.'

Now my telephone rings, and the operator says:

'Good morning, madame, will you take a personal call from London?'

Yes, I will take the call from London, but it is a business call and I am vexed to be disturbed in my enjoyment of the drama which is taking place next door. . . . She might announce something new and curious that I shall not hear. I listen a trifle absent-mindedly to what

I am being told on long distance. How very seriously men take themselves. They invariably treat me as if I were a little girl. My conversation comes to an end. I might have asked what the weather was like in London. London weather often reaches Paris a day or two later.

What a lot of time I have wasted! I arrange the pillows comfortably at my back, take up my pad and fountain-pen, and allow my memory to empty itself gently on the smooth paper. The words flow contentedly, never asking to be rearranged, dominating me —not I them. My pleasure is to be led, not to lead. I am passive, and in this essentially feminine, savouring the joys of no responsibility.

My neighbour leaves her apartment. I hear the door slam behind her and the tap of her heels in the corridor. She was so unhappy, she said, alone. I think I know now why she is so upset about the loss of the gold box. I am certain that HE must have given it to her.

Life divides itself very strangely into sections. One morning everything begins with a smile. For instance, one can quickly do one's hair, rolling it up in just the way one wants it, the hairpins sticking in perfectly, the whole thing, for once, looking very nice; and then some new addition to one's make-up proves a success, changing one's appearance agreeably at the start of the day, giving one audacity. Audacity is what a woman needs above all. She needs desperately to feel sure of herself.

Midday is striking from all the clocks in Paris, and I go down into the hall to meet Mrs Ethel Linder Reiner who has just flown in from New York. I do not know her by sight but there is no hesitation on my side as I go over to greet her. She is exquisitely dressed in the American way, has long well-shaped legs, and is admirably shod. A woman is right to neglect no seductive artifice.

We lunch together and her conversation delights me.

Mrs Reiner, having read the American edition of the story of my girlhood, liked it enough to wonder if it could be dramatized. A cable warned me of her arrival by air, but my interest in her as an individual is greater than my belief that the little Madeleine may one day be portrayed on Broadway or in Hollywood. I study her while we lunch, and I note that in spite of her femininity she immediately takes control of the situation, just as she might make detailed decisions from her office on Fifth Avenue concerning a film in Mexico, a play in New York, or anything else which came her way. She is serious and yet gay. I begin to understand this new race of American women who, in work, compete against men. Taxation being what it is, a marriage, unless one is very lucky, is no longer enough to satisfy the ambitious woman. We are almost obliged to become career women, but we are not yet, thank God, defeminized. On the contrary, it makes some of us more feminine than we might be otherwise. This one, I repeat, is adorable, her eyes cunningly underlined with an attractive dash of blue pencil. Her make-up fascinates me because its distinctively personal touch results in a type of beauty I have not yet seen in any other woman. A gold watch is fastened to her wrist by a long plaited ribbon fringed with gold, and all this shimmers and moves without that clatter of old iron which too many of us make when we wear bracelets hung with coins and charms.

She intrigues me also by favouring a semi-precious stone with which I am not very familiar—the amethyst. Amethysts are in her earrings set about with pearls, on a finger in the same way. The violet blue stone, contrasted with the milky texture of the pearls, suits her.

In a few sentences, she helps me to imagine the season on Broadway. Her descriptions are alternately acid and enthusiastic, but always penetrating. Famous names leap elegantly from her rapid tongue—Tennessee Williams, Jean-Louis Barrault, and Sir Laurence Olivier.

She reviews the political scene. We talk about sculpture. I had heard friends speak highly of her as a sculptress.

'No,' she declares, 'I have not enough talent so I took to letters. One must not waste time, if one is intelligent, doing something in which one cannot shine.'

I reflect that this woman is beautiful because she is brilliant. She is good at business, is religious, understands ideas and men, and is of the class of Clare Luce and Perle Mesta who are the new Rockefellers and the new Fords of modern America. Such women inspire youth.

Of the dramatization of books, she says:

'In the United States there is a tendency to refuse any venture that does not appear certain of success. Failures have become too costly, not only to one's banking account, but also to one's morale.'

I sit in the sunshine in the flower market of the Madeleine.

I learn that to-day is the feast day of Saint Philip. All the flower-women have chalked this fact on little blackboards above their stalls to remind those of us who may possess a Philip in the family.

At the far end of my bench, a man is dozing in the hot sunshine. Another, seated half-way between us, his walking-stick between his legs, as if he were taking the air outside his cottage in the country, is wrinkled and old. A little old woman, sweet and fragile, comes trotting along. She also sits down and begins to talk to the still, thoughtful gentleman with the stick between his legs.

'There!' she announces. 'My daughter's just had

another child.   I received a letter from her in my village, asking me to come and help.   Well, of course, I arrived by the next train, but meanwhile the husband had asked *his* mother to come, so it struck me there were too many mothers round the new baby, and here I am walking through the streets of Paris till it's time for my train to leave this evening.

'I could have gone back at midday but I was too proud.   The people in my village suppose that my daughter really needs me.   I was so flattered to be sent for from Paris!   I would hate them to know that I was not really needed.   Besides, it has never happened before that I had a whole day to waste, just walking about the streets, looking at things.   I wouldn't say that I have seen sights more extraordinary than in my own village, but never mind.   I've had lots of fun.   I think I shall relent now and help them to prepare dinner. I am hungry, and it would prevent them from saying that I was bad-tempered and hurt because of the husband's mother.   Also, I am an excellent cook.   And you?' she asks, looking up at the old man with the stick.   'How many children have you got?'

'In the name of goodness,' says the old man, tapping his stick on the ground, 'I have lost count.   Half my family went to Morocco, and as I shall never cross the sea, they have ceased to interest me.   Little children who grow up far away do not warm an old heart. They mean no more to me than a bevy of children running out of school when their lessons are over.'

'I am hungry,' repeats the old lady, as she goes off to cook her daughter's dinner.

The sleeping man wakes, stretches his limbs, and he too leaves us.   I am alone with the old gentleman with the stick.

Six o'clock has just struck, and a great many men

have come to buy flowers. They have certainly been invited out to dine, and they are buying flowers to take to their hostesses. Men on the Continent still have charming manners. They choose their flowers very quickly, pay, and hurry off. As soon as they have gone, the flower-women gather together to gossip. They wear socks, shoes with wooden heels, and black aprons with large pockets. The woman nearest me has plunged her arms, to the elbows, inside the bib of her apron so that her arms appear to be cut off. She is the most garrulous of them all. In a voice which she intends to carry four stalls away, she discusses television, and all her sentences start in much the same manner:

'And another who is very good is X, and another who is becoming rather good is Y. And this evening they are going to give us this or that, and I assure you that it's something of a programme, and for women like ourselves who have to get up at 5 a.m. to fetch the flowers at market it's a real pleasure to have all that without having to put on shoes and stockings!'

'Yes,' says another, 'I suppose we shall have to get one also. The little girl in the corner there, she's got one. The trouble is that my man doesn't hold with it.'

She nods in the direction of her man who, seated on a kitchen chair, is busy removing thorns from long-stalked roses.

'Of course,' she continues, 'I've a right to things as much as he has, given we're both in the same business, but I get worried if he doesn't think the same way as I do about things.'

Her man looks up and says quietly:

'I'm not against the thing as a thing, but I do so like to play cards with the boys at the local café in the evening, and when she has got her TV set, I know quite well I shan't be able to join them any more. My little fun in life will have gone. Of course, if it isn't me, it will be the others. What my dad did and my grandad—well, it'll all be finished. And it's true,' he adds, laughing good-humouredly, 'it's true as you see me plucking the thorns off these roses that I fight against having one of those things, but I know that when the boys all slink off one after the other, because their wives have bought TV sets, then it'll be my turn, because there'll be nobody left to play cards with me in the café.'

'You poor darling, you're mad!' says his wife.

A woman comes to buy an immense bunch of daisies, and out of respect for her all the stall-holders remain politely silent. When she has gone the women get together again, and a new subject comes up for discussion. A girl who recently came to learn their business lacked patience, and, what was much more serious, she was rough with the flowers. She assassinated them. None of the older women could make her understand.

'The fortune she cost me in arum lilies!' exclaims the woman who has just sold the daisies. 'When I found her with a decapitated bloom, she would say: "I didn't do it on purpose, and these arum lilies have such a horrible smell that I can't understand why anybody should want to buy them!" Imagine! Imagine her saying that! Not only did she murder my lovely flowers but she insulted them as well.'

'That's the spirit of the new age,' says another. 'They won't trouble to learn. Their insults are a form of self-defence.'

A No. 42 bus takes me within a few yards of the Plaza-Athénée.

If one feels that the bus is going to be at all full, one tears off a numbered ticket at the bus stop. This is a form of queueing without standing in a queue, but our republic is a land of privileges. When the bus arrives, long before the ticket-holders have a chance of boarding it, the conductor comes out on his platform and calls for those who have priority cards, men who were wounded in the war, mothers of large families, expectant mothers, those ex-soldiers, poor things, who were gassed in the First World War, a member of the Resistance during the Second World War, and so on. In spite of all this one generally manages to find room on the back platform where people stand up, lean over the rails, and are much more friendly. The conductor hooks a leather lanyard across the entrance, pulls down a notice which reads FULL, and disappears inside his bus to collect the fares.

By the time he has come to take my ticket, we have reached the Rond Point. He looks round at the wide avenue, the flowers in their beds, and the chestnut-trees in all their glory, and says:

'It's lovely here, isn't it? Where are you getting off?'

'At the corner of the Avenue Montaigne.'

'Yes,' he says again. 'It's so lovely, one can hardly believe it. It's even more lovely than being in the country. I would give anything in the world to live around here.'

'Oh, I know!' I exclaim. 'You don't need to tell me that.'

'You mean you live round here?' he asks. 'How on earth did you find a flat?'

'Oh, I live among the chimney-pots,' I laugh. 'Right at the top of the Plaza-Athénée.'

'What!' he exclaims, 'and you travel by bus!'

'I'm lucky there's this bus that brings me to the door.'

'Ah!' he says. 'You had me guessing a moment. You mean that you work here?'

'Well,' I answer, 'I certainly work.'

He looks relieved.

'You know,' he says, 'this problem of finding a flat gives me nightmares.   Here I am crossing Paris from end to end, seeing apartments everywhere, and saying to myself how excellently almost any of them would suit me, and getting back to the depot no better off than when I left it in the morning.   Three children already, and we still have to live with my wife's people!   Look at all those hotels and offices—no, it's not the hotels I mind so much.   Those monster offices, those are the things that make me mad.   Thousands and thousands of them.   All the centre of the city.   Nothing but offices, offices.   How I loathe them!   I'd set fire to the whole lot.   There now,' he adds, smiling, 'this is where you get off.   Take care you don't slip getting down with those high heels.'

Oh, how right he was!   How lovely is the Avenue Montaigne!

I am called on the telephone from Versailles.

The Begum Aga Khan asks me to lunch next day with herself and the prince at the Restaurant de la Pérouse.   She is so sweet to me that I am ready to cry. I feel somehow that I have no right to be living in my attic.   I wonder what has happened to my neighbour's gold box?   If ever I am introduced to her I shall have to ask her to tell me the end of the story.

CHAPTER XII

THE RESTAURANT DE LA PÉROUSE is very old and made up of small public and private rooms reminiscent of the novels of 1900, when it was fashionable for rich men to attach a delightful importance to eating and drinking, and falling in and out of love. There is romance also in the restaurant's situation, for it is on the quay of the Augustinian saints (*Le Quai des Saints-Augustins*) from which one may see the Law Courts and Notre Dame. I am glad to be a few moments early. I read a great many novels in my girlhood about assignations in the private rooms of restaurants and in small apartments known as *garçonnières* kept up by rich men solely for that purpose. The *garçonnière* no longer exists in Paris because in these days of increasing population and housing shortage, it would be considered anti-social for a man, even if he could afford it, to immobilize an extra apartment for the pleasure of meeting his mistress in it once or twice a week. The motor-car, of course, has come in time to serve more or less the same purpose. The gentleman who proposes to drive you out into the country in his roadster is virtually repeating an age-old invitation, but it is less poetical, less romantic, perhaps—at any rate, in the eyes of French people—than the small, mysterious apartment where the lover waited impatiently for the lady of his dreams who would arrive, her features hidden by a veil, her silk dress made voluminous by a multitude of seductive petticoats.

Ah! Here comes the Aga Khan with his lovely Begum!

The Begum is in sapphire blue and wears a large diamond ring. She tells me about the ball of the Little White Beds which is one of the most important social functions of the season. This year it was held at the Moulin Rouge, and for the first time was televised. She and the prince arrived, sat down, and were then asked to make their entry all over again because the television camera had not functioned properly; and the Aga Khan, who is amused by everything in life, from winning the Derby to listening to feminine chatter, immediately obeyed.

We discuss plays. I ask their opinion of the *Heure Éblouissante*, and to my delight the Begum says:

'My instinct now is to go to plays which are recommended to me by women. I am seldom disappointed. Women in recommending plays eliminate, I find, those that treat of sordid crimes and all those pretentious discussions on social problems. They prefer love stories. What a relief! How right they are! Love is not the prerogative of the rich. The poor girl dreams of little else. She finds its sunshine just as warm. This is a fact many people forget. My husband and I have a passion for the theatre. This evening, for instance, we are going to the Théâtre Français to see Racine's *Andromaque*. This is my choice. I only wonder if my husband will like it.'

The Aga Khan smiles. His wife knows that he will like everything she likes. The whole world is a play for him. I tell him what a lot of things I have forgotten about the city of my birth, and how I explore it avidly, either on foot or on the swaying rear platform of a bus; and because I know that everything amuses him, I say:

'The front of a Paris bus is just the same as any other

bus, in London, Buenos Aires, or New York, but the platform at the back, with the rail over which one can lean watching the cobbles fly past as if they were little white horses on the sea, that is to be found nowhere else in the world.

'This is the third class where we all stand up. When the driver swerves round corners we clutch at whatever we can, breathing the good air of the streets, the drains of the medieval ones, the flowers in the flower market, the garlic of our neighbours, and because we are standing up, not sitting down in a formal, well-brought-up way, we quickly talk to one another. This morning I tried to interest a puppy which a woman was carrying in a basket, but I felt that I was being looked at from behind. It is amazing how one knows. I knew also, without turning, which of the passengers it was, a young man, much younger than myself. "Really!" he exclaimed, as the bus jolted over the cobble-stones of the quays. "How this bus does shake!" His hand moved along the rail and quickly folded itself over mine, and then I turned, and saw a tender, protecting look in his eyes!'

'How lovely!' says the Begum. 'The flattering look or word from a man who simply has no idea who you are is a lovely thing.'

'Yes,' I agree, 'for when one is the tiniest bit known, a man who is well brought up, especially in Paris, will always try to say—even though he does not believe a word of it—that one is either pretty or well dressed, or, failing either of these things, that one is intelligent, but the other . . . that is what gives one a lovely feeling.'

'We left the Moulin Rouge,' says the Begum, 'in the small hours. The ball was a great success. A crowd stood outside watching the people get into their cars, and as we passed a man's voice exclaimed: "Ah! *There* is what I call a beautiful woman!" I was enchanted, delighted. I think perhaps when one is very young, one does not recognize the value of such compliments— as the one made to you just now in the bus, and to me by the unknown man in the crowd. No, on the contrary, one feels insulted. In truth one is too touchy, too nervous, too sensitive. For instance, one day when I was twenty, waiting to cross the street, a drover, passing with his heavy horse and cart, looked me up and down and exclaimed:

'"What a lovely racehorse!"

'I was furious. I felt annihilated by this remark which I took to be merely vulgar, and it was only when I married, and later took an interest in racehorses, that I discovered what he had meant, and what a splendid compliment the drover had paid me.'

'You have certainly made amends,' said the Aga Khan. 'Anybody would think that you two women were exclusively interested in the compliments you pick up in the street!'

He adores the company of women. His eyes are alight with pleasure. He was brought up by women and is vastly amused by our disclosures, our laughter, our sentimentality, but he has suddenly decided that he does not want to go to the Théâtre Français this evening and so the tickets are handed to me. The Aga Khan calls for his car and drives off. The Begum and I walk a little way along the bank of the Seine. We look at the second-hand books.

'The Aga Khan reminds me of an adorable cat!' I say suddenly.

'He is exactly like a cat,' answers the Begum. 'He allows himself to be amused, stroked—then suddenly he has had enough, and goes off on his own. He is of an independent and proud nature, exactly like a Persian cat.'

She accompanies me back to the Plaza-Athénée

where we find Véra Korène, the famous actress of the
Comédie Française, in the hall. We introduce ourselves,
and I ask Véra Korène if she is playing in *Andromaque*
this evening. Yes, she answers, she will play the role of
Hermione, daughter of Helen and Menelaus, and will I
not come to visit her during the interval?

'Now,' says the Begum to me, 'take me up to your
attic, and show me the Eiffel Tower.'

She stands delightedly by the open french windows,
looking out across the green and grey roofs of Paris
towards the Eiffel Tower, and almost like a little girl
she says:

'Wouldn't it be terrible if they took it away from
us?'

She turns and picks up a book on my dressing-table.
During my wanderings I had discovered a copy of *Le
Passé*, a very favourite play by Porto Riche. The first
performance was, I think, in 1911 but I still found it
fresh and beautifully constructed. I had bought it in an
arcade behind the rue Vivienne, where the woman who
owned the place told me that business was becoming a
little less good every year.

'The Parisian used to be a great walker,' she said.
'He would walk up and down the boulevards, have a
coffee, talk to his friends, and then browse in the shops.
Narrow streets delighted him. He would always be on
the look out for something quaint and interesting.
Books were his passion. He would spend hours in a
bookshop and end by taking away some volume that
amused him. Think, madame, we have been here for
one hundred and fifteen years! My family have sold
books in this very shop since the reign of Louis Philippe.
Lamartine, Balzac, Gautier, Baudelaire, have stood where
you are standing. Offenbach with his pince-nez and
side-whiskers came in and out humming an air. That
is something to think about, is it not? Alas, people do

H

not saunter any more. They transport themselves from the outskirts of Paris to the centre, and from the centre back to the outskirts as fast as they possibly can. The older customers slowly disappear. There are no young ones to take their place. And yet we do not close during the lunch hour and we remain open till nine at night, sometimes later. These 'digests' are a real curse, and what an ugly name! They are about the only things we can sell. They tell you a bit about everything, so that you have no need to read anything. Real books, the good, comfortable books to handle and to read, the friendly book to have by you always—the books are the losers, madame. And so what do you make of all this talk about popular education? Still, we mustn't grumble. My family, during one hundred and fifteen years, must have disseminated a great deal of knowledge and pleasure, and how many people can say as much?'

The Begum has gone, taking *Le Passé* with her, so I, in turn, am helping to sow the good seed. The woman at the bookshop also sold me a novel of the same period as the play, but I find it rather dull.

As I go to the Théâtre Français with a former cavalry officer and his wife, we arrive long before the play starts. Some men attach great importance to the clock. I respect and envy them, but I find myself constantly attaching greater importance to whatever it is that prevents me from being on time.

I start by criticizing *Andromaque*. These Greeks, seen through the eyes of the great Racine, courted tragedy for such seemingly futile reasons. I even ask myself if the classics are now out of date. However, these bloodthirsty legends, I reflect, have lived two thousand years, whereas I am having trouble just now in reading a novel written forty years ago.

The acting is admirable. There is no such finish to be seen anywhere in the world. The female characters are full of dignity and grace in these Greek costumes that grow upon one. Véra Korène, with her long blonde tresses, has finally succeeded in getting Pyrrhus murdered by Orestes, and now will have nothing more to do with him because he has obeyed her cruel command. She loved Pyrrhus and accordingly prepares to kill herself across the dead body of the man she loved, whilst Andromache, Hector's wife, has rid herself of Pyrrhus whom she only married to save her son.

I now hurry to seek out Hermione in her dressing-room.

I do not need to go so far.

Hermione, restored to life, is leaning over a banister in deep conversation with Orestes, discussing his acting, tempering her criticism with delicate compliments and wise advice; he, extremely respectful, shining eyes widened with make-up, a narrow beard running in a half-circle round his chin, looking very youthful. Of all these Greek men I found him the most sympathetic in the play.

'There!' she says finally. 'Good night.'

He bends over her extended hand, and placing his lips with rare delicacy over her lovely fingers, takes his leave. She then, with the dignity of her high position in the historic theatre, invites us into her dressing-room.

I follow her with a sense of my awkwardness in this strange world. She handles her long white dress with the same cunning as she did on the stage, whereas I am in great fear of stepping on the train. I feel like a young girl up from the country. Her dressing-room surprises me by its beauty, for being a life member she can make a second home of her dressing-room. Her other home is, in fact, close to mine on the top of the Plaza-Athénée.

This one reminds me of a Watteau fan and yet its decorations are modern, but all the famous classical roles she has played are represented round the walls—Phaedra, Pasiphae, Andromache . . . and I know not how many others. There is no glare. On the contrary, it is almost dark. It is charming, like a medieval religious book with hand-painted pictures. A door hidden in the wall swings open and reveals, like some secret chamber of Catherine de' Medici, an admirable dressing-table with all the make-up necessary for stage and town. Like Mignon, in the land of oranges, I exclaim inwardly: 'This is where I would like to live!'

As to some Greek goddess, designs for costumes are brought to her. A young Italian, small, fine of feature, dressed in contrasting colours, submits designs. One of them is for an eighteenth-century play; the other for a Greek one. A young woman is just behind him, his wife or his sister, who encourages him, speaking at the right moment on his behalf, pointing out what is excellent in his drawings; but indeed the great actress is not difficult to convince, for the drawings are magnificent, amazingly mature for so young a man, and he is suddenly delighted, for she has said she will keep them and discuss them with the producer in the morning.

I say I am curious to know what she has found to criticize in the performance of Orestes.

'Very little,' she says, smiling. 'He gave a very good performance this evening. He told me he had been playing tennis all the afternoon and was tired. That was excellent for his acting, for he is very young and apt to be a little impetuous.'

Pieces of magnificent white jersey, white as snow, are stretched across the actress's couch.

'Yes,' she says. 'They were draped over me in a fitting this afternoon and within half an hour I had a very beautiful chlamys. The material is lovely, isn't it?'

This superb actress does indeed look very well in white, and then her language, the words she employs to express the simplest, commonest things, her admirable diction, fill one with respect. How immense is the intelligence of a woman who, like this one, has reached the very pinnacle of her hard profession, a successor to the Duse, to Sarah Bernhardt; and one realizes how intoxicating, how engrossing, it must be. And then I think of Orestes on his tennis-court. How charming to have a son who played Orestes!

CHAPTER XIII

NOW FOR THE children's party. The house where it is taking place is much larger than any left in the hands of private people in London. Capitals, reputedly poor, like Paris and Madrid, give one occasional glimpses of what it must have been like to be wealthy in the nineteenth century. There is a porter's lodge, a courtyard in front, a large quiet garden behind, and servants to address you in the third person. 'If madame will give herself the trouble to step this way. . . .' I think it is perfectly charming, but then I always loved reading about it in novels and when, on very rare occasions, I step into this elevated world, I feel like a little girl being shown something delightfully unreal.

This house belongs to a widow of considerable taste. A person can be endowed, of course, with excellent taste which is not necessarily acceptable to oneself, but in this house I would gladly live, and what is more I would be able to find within it the intensity necessary to my well-being, for there are pictures, books, the sort of tapestries and hangings which I like. I admire particularly a vase about two feet tall made in the form of an iris. Two petals of this noble flower are bent back just as one sees in a real garden, and the whole is a most delicate shade of mauve, warmed and brought to life by a vein of gold.

I enter the drawing-room. The children, seated at a number of small tables, are being waited upon by a footman wearing white gloves. My eyes look with delight upon small heads bobbing up and down, some with

paper hats, while adorable puffed sleeves make the little
girls look like seagulls poised on the foreshore.   In the
distance I see a row of nurses discreetly watching their
charges, and some very elegant mothers, extremely
Faubourg Saint-Germain, that is to say, of a proud and
exclusive aristocracy whose members do not make
friends with people outside their own social world.
They are elegant but ugly, and even their elegance is
distinctive, for it is not the elegance of smart clothes,
but that which results from many generations of aristo-
cratic breeding and enables them to look different
from others.

While the children are having tea, cushions are being
placed on the carpet at the far end of the long room
whose tall french windows open out on the garden.   A
conjuror and a puppet show have been engaged.

A little boy who tried to catch a goldfish in the tiny
pond in the garden is brought in by his nurse who will
hurry him upstairs to dry his blouse with an iron.   The
garden is full of coloured balloons tied by silk threads
to the bushes and shrubs.   They dance amusingly in
the variable gusts of hot wind blowing across the house-
tops from the direction of the Champs Élysées.   The
conjuror, the footman, and one father are the only men.

The children have finished tea and leave the tables.
The little girls have marvellous dresses, beautiful
smocks, superb embroidery, adorable petticoats, long
hair tied back in the horse's tail fashion, or cut short in
a poodle crop to resemble their mothers.   That is the
triumph of being a little girl.   One is already a grown
woman.   One is as elegant as one's mother.   One is as
conscious of one's womanhood as one will be to-morrow
when one is quite grown up.   Boys are either sweet or
gawky.   Nothing foretells as yet the distinctive appearance of to-morrow's man.   The boy seems to go back-
wards in looks and intelligence to give a bigger leap

forwards when the moment is right. We are so much cleverer when we are girls, but in adult life few of us can compete against the exceptional man.

Two small sisters come and settle beside me. We are friends. The party is being held in honour of one of them whose birthday it is. It is also the birthday of their little white dog. During tea the two sisters smiled at me. They were the only ones to break through the wall of voices and laughter which divided me from the rest of the room. They wear hydrangea-blue, embroidered cotton dresses with wide satin sashes of ruby red. As soon as they sit on the cushioned floor their dresses spread out round them like huge powder-puffs, the tips of their shoes peeping out like rabbits' ears. The elder sister is six and her maternal instincts cause her to take up her little sister and arrange her on her lap, encircling her tightly with tiny white arms, as she would lovingly hold a doll, and though the conjuror has started to pull things out of a hat, she continues to clasp the living doll, keeping quite still for fear of disturbing her. She will be elegant but also, I reflect, an excellent mother, and I derive great joy in watching the way she peeps from time to time into her small sister's face to see how she is enjoying the show.

The conjuror goes on with his tricks but the smaller of my two friends remains as quiet as the older one who, of course, is as proud as a queen. I am sure that the little sister finds the big sister's arms infinitely comforting. Now we have the puppet show. Young voices are raised. All these children are bilingual and they jump from English into French with complete ease. In neither language have they a trace of accent. They are enjoying themselves in a quietly sophisticated way. Their laughter is already elegant, perfectly modulated and controlled, and there is never an unnecessary or ugly gesture. Clearly they are accustomed to being in rich drawing-rooms, surrounded by lovely things, and it will be some years yet before they learn that there are poor children whose ways are very different from theirs. The lovely drawing-room suddenly fades and I see before me Victor Hugo's house with the little girl who has blackened her lips and chin with shoe-shine.

The party is over, and the nurses step forward to claim their charges. The gravelled courtyard is full of cars with liveried chauffeurs. The children very politely say good-bye to their hostess, and then to one another. Politeness is a lovely thing. The children will meet again at the seaside, in country houses on the banks of the Loire, and next January in Switzerland where they will learn to ski while their mothers continue to talk slimming, fashions, and the latest journeys. They will welcome one another with the words: 'Oh, my dear, fancy meeting you here!' though they invariably go to the same places at the same time.

How intensely do the Latin countries cling to a way of life that elsewhere seems feudal. Having been poor myself, I am less anxious to condemn the rich. They have more qualities than they themselves are aware of. This children's party must have cost a great deal of money, and then it will doubtless be repeated at each child's birthday, but I am not impressed by the cost. I doubt if money any longer adds up to anything. Does anybody ever give to you or me what something that did not happen might have cost? Am I jealous? I feel no jealousy. If these children have easy beginnings, remember that the little boys will have to go to school, far from their homes, be shut up in colleges, herded into the army, robbed of freedom. I thank God I was a girl and poor enough not to be removed by force from the great throb of the everyday street scene. Am I not fortunate to have squeezed out of life, while other girls

were playing hockey, the whole poignant range of
human emotions?

How lovely not to be in a motor-car but walking
briskly down the Champs Élysées! The shops where
they sell stuffs and materials have become absolute
palaces. I spend hours in them. I am bewitched by
these magnificent fabrics made of I know not what. I
also enjoy listening to the salesgirls who, having asked
me what I want, and finding that I want nothing, group
themselves together again, and talk—fashions and
love! They convey the impression that nothing else
matters. How wise they are! How utterly delightful!
I buy nothing. In Paris I am too busy to sew.
There is so much to see and to hear. Thus, for the
first time in my life, I hardly thread a needle except to
replace a button or to mend the hem of a skirt. In
imagination, however, I make the loveliest things,
dresses that—lucky things—will never be out of date or
grow out of favour. Thus, full of delightful thoughts,
I hurry along the Champs Élysées. There are perfumery shops that set my blood on fire. By frequenting
them I am able, at small expense, to make a major
change each day in the appearance of my face. This is
not possible in London. I would be intimidated. I
would not have the courage to go out into Piccadilly one
morning looking quite different, for to change one's
appearance successfully one must make a habit of it.
In Paris it is in the very air one breathes. One feels
ashamed to go about looking the same as yesterday. I
notice that the hairdressers' and the shoe shops are
always busy, but my greatest temptation is to buy a
hand-bag. There is a shop in front of which I have
been stopping for a few moments every afternoon. I
am delighted both by the bags and by the name of the
owner—for he is called Borgia. Now, at last, I will go

in. I inspect, I touch, and I open the most exquisite works of art. Each is prettier and more cunningly made than the one before. Alas, I cannot afford them.

'Madame,' says the salesgirl, 'I admit that these crocodile bags are expensive and that you would need as much money to buy four of them as to buy a good motor-car. On the other hand these bags are hand made by specialized craftsmen, whereas the motor-car would probably be mass produced. Is it not fair that the product of a man's individual skill should be relatively more expensive than the product of a machine? So, madame, may I not tempt you?'

May she not tempt me?

I am tempted at every step—materials, perfumes, make-up, shoes. . . .

As I open my bedroom door I hear a flutter of wings. A very young sparrow, attracted by the bread and milk on my balcony, has come into the room and is banging his poor beak against the mirrors. I take him in my hands, my first little Parisian baby sparrow, and stroke him gently. He looks relieved. He remains still but his heart continues to beat very fast. After a few moments I take him to the balcony and show him the roofs of the town.

Swiftly and happily he flies away.

CHAPTER XIV

HERE IS A BUS that will take me across the Seine and along the quays as far as the Law Courts, but as I am tired I shall take a seat inside. A coloured woman from Martinique, that romantic French island in the West Indies, smiles and squeezes herself against the window to make room for me. I try to remember what they taught me as a little girl at school about Martinique. I think it produces sugar-cane, tobacco, rum, coffee, and what my geography described as 'the most delicious fruit.' As a young woman I once went cruising in the West Indies, but fruit there matures too quickly. It is not so good as the fruit in Europe. I must talk to this Martiniquaise. I smile back and ask her what she has been doing.

'Oh, madame, I have been to see the Eiffel Tower, because when I return to my own land they will all ask me about it, and though I have seen the top of the tower very often, I was not at all certain what the base was like. And so, madame, as I hope soon to return to my own people, I have been near enough to touch it.'

'What makes you return to Martinique?'

'Oh, madame, I am always cold, and every year I feel the cold more. My master and mistress are very good. They are arranging for me to go home to Saint-Pierre. They understand how disagreeable it is for me to feel cold, because when they visit Saint-Pierre, where they found me, they are always too warm. I came to Paris to look after their little girl, madame. She is as lovely as the sun but, alas, like the sun in the sky, she goes to bed in the evening, and as soon as she is no longer with me I feel the cold.'

Her simplicity is touching and I would like to cry. She obviously feels that I am her friend, for she goes on:

'So when I am alone in the evenings, madame, I pray and I knit. I have knitted stacks of pullovers which, I suppose, will be no good to me when I am back home.'

She has an umbrella with a plexyglass handle, and while she is talking to me she amuses herself by putting her black fingers with her pink nails behind the plexyglass, which makes them look larger, blacker, and pinker than they really are.

'Oh, this is where I leave the bus, madame. Goodbye, madame.'

'Good-bye, little Martiniquaise. Have a good journey home.'

A young woman climbs quickly into the bus. Now where have I seen her before? I remember especially her rather sulky mouth, but how elegant she is! What a lovely figure! In spite of a natural inclination towards jealousy, I must concede that she is a fine girl.

She crosses the entire length of the bus and sits down just in front of me, but what surprises me is that nobody takes the slightest notice of her. Am I the only person to be aware that she is rather out of the ordinary? If only I could recall what made me notice that sulky, proud mouth! Why, of course. It all comes back to me! This lovely girl who is attracting no attention whatever in the bus is a Christian Dior mannequin, and at the show the other day all the buyers were enthusiastic about her as she paraded with haughty insolence in the loveliest dresses of the spring collection.

Is this a lesson in humility? Does it mean that a lovely woman removed from her environment loses much of her attraction? Perhaps, but a great deal less

so than the president of a hundred million dollar cor-
poration who might decide to leave his Cadillac and
travel by bus. At least the girl remains beautiful. If
I had the choice I would a thousand times rather be she.

As I am a full hour too early for my appointment, I
will jump off and continue my journey on foot. Here
is the Châtelet which, like Drury Lane, stages magnificent
musicals. This is where the Boucry girl with whom I
was brought up at Clichy won success as a dancer. I
would have loved to see her, but I used to think of the
Châtelet and the Folies Bergères as places beneath the
notice of earnest young women like myself. I was not
attracted by shows with lovely girls, which I imagined
to be only for foreigners who did not speak the language,
and business men trying to forget their wives. To be
a show-girl oneself might have been charming but to
spend an evening watching them would have made me
miserable. I would have compared myself unfavourably
with every girl on the stage and by midnight I would
have been ready to throw myself into the Seine.

The sky darkens and rain pours down. A little man
about to cross the street gallantly takes me under his
umbrella and asks me where I am going. As the Bazar
de l'Hôtel de Ville is opposite I leave him at the first
door and find myself in the book department, where to
my delight I discover a treatise by a Mme Zézina on
how to foretell the future with playing-cards.

Unfortunately the book is new so that my reading is
continually being left in suspense where I cannot finish
a phrase owing to the pages being uncut. However,
the introduction is excellent and the book appears to
be written in a clever and serious way.

Certain days of the week, I learn, are inauspicious for
telling one's fortune. Monday, the day of the moon,
is excellent provided that it falls on an uneven date,
Wednesday is suitable for inquiring into the outcome

of financial operations, it is the day of Mercury, god of commerce, but Friday is the day of Venus and we must therefore set aside this day for our amorous problems which, if we are women, will be far the most important.

One must on no account read cards on Sunday, or any feast day or public holiday, and this includes 14th July, in spite of the fact that the storming of the Bastille was a revolutionary, not a religious act. The cards, if one disobeys this law, will lie or remain silent. The best day of all is Friday the 13th, because the 13th is the symbol of good fortune.

This book is well worth one hundred and ninety francs. I shall take it home and cut the pages at leisure, and besides, the sun has suddenly come out brilliantly, making the electric lighting in the store appear dim and yellow. I pass quickly through the stationery department which, for some reason, is full of young ecclesiastics wearing Alpine berets, and though the beret suits their dark skins, I deplore the passing of the medieval hat with its wide and gracious brim that is seen only occasionally now in Spain and in Italy.

I cross the Seine whose swift waters are deep and murky. Rain has come down in torrents during the last few days. I am reminded that every evening, after a quick look at my horoscope which has been proving itself quite unbelievably accurate, I read in the paper that some unfortunate has thrown himself over one of these bridges.

I have now reached the parvis of Notre Dame. The sky is romantically dark again and I think of Quasimodo, the hunchback of Victor Hugo's great tale, and I am full of wonder for the genius of this novelist and poet who was able to make us see so vividly, on this sacred spot, a beggars' meet that he himself had never known. Over these rough stones Quasimodo followed the beautiful Esmeralda, and even as I look, reconstructing the past, I see a great crowd hurrying, pressed tightly together and yet silent, as if they are ghosts superimposing the pictures of my imagining on the realities of the present hour. I feel myself irresistibly drawn towards the dark, moving crowd, and I am not sure whether I am anxious to lose my identity within it, or continue to follow Quasimodo in his quest for Esmeralda. Then suddenly engulfed in it, moving with it, I reach a heavy portal, very high and dark, making a picturesque half-circle above which I read: HÔTEL-DIEU—Liberté, Égalité, Fraternité.

The doors swing open and I realize that this is visiting-day at the oldest hospital in Paris, originally built in the seventh century by Saint Landri, Bishop of Paris, on the very parvis on which a few moments ago I was walking; burned down and rebuilt just before the French Revolution; pulled down and built a third time during the years that straddled the Franco-Prussian War of 1870, a few hundred yards away, on the present site.

I now look round me with a greater awareness of the present, and I notice that most of the men and women composing this crowd carry gifts, bags of food, or bouquets of flowers. Some are gay, many sad, but as they move slowly along the cold, damp ground, they talk in low tones as if given sudden hope by the opening of the doors. I am carried with them into an enormous yard in which I see a great number of crutches and wheel-chairs, and over us looms the architecture of an age when men went to battle with horses, sabres, and plumed helmets, and doctors knew practically nothing about preventing or curing disease.

The building forms an immense rectangle with central courts and cloisters, rather dark, very still, with stone benches along the walls. I find myself on the men's side, and peeping through a glass door I can see the wards in which some patients have their families grouped at their bedside, while others are alone, reading. Each ward bears the name of a saint. This is Saint Charles. I see billowing waves of white beds, and incongruously amongst all this white, a negro, alone, sitting up in bed, his arms inert like two black sticks on the white sheet. Now, there is something I have never seen before—a negro in bed.

Here is the founder's ward, the ward of Saint Landri, with windows so high that all I see is sparrows hopping from bar to bar.

In the cloisters a grey cat, whose flanks are so heavy that she will soon be a mother, wants me to stroke her. She purrs and miaows. A door opens, releasing a delicious smell of steak and fried potatoes. A nurse, plate in hand, calls the cat who throws up her tail, utters a short cry of pleasure, and advances with slow, dignified tread towards the kitchen. The smell of fried potatoes takes possession of the cloisters now. What seemed grey and old-fashioned has become warm and comforting, so that one feels that there might be compensations for the eighty-year-old walls, the tall, barred windows, and the strange stillness of the inner courts.

I walk to the far end of the cloisters, and come upon the women's side, and I am curiously relieved as if I had been trespassing and was now safely back with members of my own sex. There is the Sainte Monique for surgical cases, and . . . ah! I knew I would find her! Here is the Sainte Madeleine, *my* ward! A sweet little girl, sitting up in bed, is talking to two women, doubtless her mother and her grandmother, and she must be making excellent progress, for she is amusing them mightily, and through the glass window I can see her horse's tail coiffure bobbing up and down and her lips moving. Even as I stand looking at this scene, another cat, much younger, rubs against my stockings.

I

She is as grey as the grey walls of the cloisters, a daughter perhaps of the old one who so soon will have a new batch of kittens.

Now I am in the *patio* with a hot sun, between showers, deepening the vivid colour of a thousand scarlet geraniums which surround a statue of Dupuytren, the celebrated surgeon of Napoleonic times. History assails me on every side, the more recent evoking little gulps of lived-through remembrance, like the long lists of young doctors killed during the war of 1914–18 when I was a little girl, and I am struck by the pure French of the names compared with the pitiful list of Cahens, Weils, and Ormanskys massacred by the German invaders between 1940 and 1945, for no other reason than that they were members of the martyred race. How many clever brains and useful lives were cut down, too briefly mourned and now quite forgotten!

I leave the hospital and come upon a magnificent flower market with rows of pink and blue hydrangeas on the cobbles, massed geraniums, fuchsias nodding delicate drooping heads with Japanese grace, and red roses that fill the air with heavy scent, but the flower-women have withdrawn into their glass cabins in which I see them cooking steaks and frying potatoes which will be copiously washed down with red wine.

All along the Quay of the Flowers and the Quay of Corsica, plants hide the cobble-stones with riots of odoriferous colour, and I look with amazement at this wonderful carpet which might have been conjured up by a fairy at the touch of her magic wand for a queen to walk triumphantly over undulating, living flowers.

In and out fly sparrows, softly flows the Seine. On a marble plaque I read:

A police-officer was shot here by the Germans
—August 1944

A vase contains half a dozen cornflowers, but the sun, falling upon them, gives them such an intensity that momentarily they out-colour the thousands of rich blooms all round them. Clocks on medieval buildings strike two, and I am suddenly hungry. I will have something at this brasserie, a plate of cold roast beef, gherkins, and a glass of Beaujolais. Rested and refreshed, I climb more serenely the steps of the Law Courts.

I have a rendezvous outside the barristers' changing-room, and I am amused by the frantic coming and going. To my surprise there are nearly as many women barristers as men. They are of all ages, and of varying appearance, though the majority are small and dark. Others are fat and much older than I would have expected. One is the image of a street singer I knew as a girl in Montmartre. Her hair is dyed bright straw but she has beautiful legs and is proud of them, for they are balanced on very high heels. A few are not at all elegant and walk in the funniest way, nodding their heads like puppets in a ballet. The men are more accustomed to these barristers' robes, but their faces automatically acquire a studied gravity which makes them look like actors or clergymen. From now on I shall probably claim that the clergymen and the actors look like barristers. One must admit, however, that the habit makes the monk, for when I see the men come out without their flowing robes, I do not need to be told that they are still waiting for fame. They are shabby and there is dandruff on their coats.

Some are very young. Some are very old. One has a white beard like the pictures of Anatole France. Most of the men wear the discreet ribbons of their decorations, and these add little splashes of colour to the black robes. One very young man must have had an exceptionally fine war record. He is talking very gaily to an older barrister who has the blind man's white stick, and when the conversation is over, the blind barrister moves off following the curve of the wall. He touches lightly with his stick a group of men reading something on a notice-board and apologizes. Soon he reaches a door that is familiar to him, for he grasps the handle firmly, and opening it disappears. I am very moved, but here is a barrister with an arm amputated at the elbow. He keeps his brief-case under the stump so that he can freely offer his hand in greeting, as is the custom in France when friends meet. Men are continually shaking hands in an affectionate and fraternal manner.

Ah! Here is my friend.

CHAPTER XV

THE NAME of Maître Delauney came up in conversation with a woman barrister at the Law Courts. She was surprised that I did not know him because he was a product of Clichy who was distinguishing himself in the legal profession. Simone Vardon exclaimed: 'But of course you must meet him!' and arranged that I should call on him in the rue de Lisbonne.

A district of Paris behind the Gare Saint-Lazare is known as the Quartier de l'Europe. The streets are named after various capital cities—the rue de Londres, the rue de Rome, the rue de Madrid, the rue de Bukarest, the rue de Stalingrad, the rue de Lisbonne. Maître Delauney has a very spacious apartment. He had said: 'Come early before I start work.' The maid shows me into a very fine drawing-room whose walls are dazzlingly white and bare, walls with no past and no memories. There are no knick-knacks, no framed photographs, but there is a splendid carpet and the cushions in the arm-chairs are new and blown out as they should be. The sofa is beautifully upholstered. 'Clearly,' I reflect, 'this is a long way from Clichy. The legal profession has pecuniary advantages.' The maid asks my name and says:

'If madame will be seated, I will tell Maître Delauney that madame is here and I will fetch her dossier.'

'There is no dossier,' I exclaim. 'I am not a client but . . . well, it's not that sort of visit.'

'Madame means that it is her first visit,' she answers

brightly. 'Maître Delauney will soon establish her dossier.'

She smiles encouragingly, and I feel self-conscious as if my features portrayed the avowal of a crime or a desire to have my husband followed. The maid disappears and a few minutes later Maître Delauney, in appearance very much the French politician, enters and asks me to follow him.

His study is as it should be, packed with books. There is a biography of Maître Henri-Robert, the famous barrister, legal books, serious books. The master sits down at his desk. The wall behind him is a solid mass of books bound in a severe shade of leather. I cannot help imagining a photograph in some serious newspaper, with the caption: 'This is the latest picture of the master in his study,' and I recall certain aspects of *Three Guineas* in which Virginia Woolf laughs in a feminine way at the vanity of famous men. I am intimidated. I am aware that the man behind the imposing desk has, from the very start of the interview, established the superiority of his sex. I can do nothing about it. It is absurd but I blush and feel stupid. I am, in his presence, merely a woman—and not a woman with the academic background necessary to hold my own against the precise phrases which I expect at any moment to issue from his mouth. How much more at ease I was in Véra Korène's dressing-room at the Comédie Française!

He sits very solemnly at his desk writing down my name, my address in Paris, my address in London. The little maid was right. He is compiling a dossier. I derive some satisfaction from his obvious difficulty in spelling my London address. This restores, to some extent, the balance of power. I may be a woman, I may have no university degrees, but I am at home in two languages. He puts down his pen and speaks, and the words are indeed carefully chosen and precise. They ring out as they should do. He at least is not nervous. He is the man.

Well, I must try to explain my business.

'Maître,' I begin, addressing him by the title of 'master' which, with a barrister, is common usage in France. 'It is merely that, as Simone Vardon, Mireille Maroger's sister, has told you, we are both children of Clichy. Simone added that at one time you were even a little envious of the pastor's brilliant family.'

'But of course I was,' he answers volubly. 'Just consider that those people were extraordinarily good-looking. They enjoyed excellent health. They knew how to express themselves in perfect French. There were so many brilliant members of the family that they virtually composed their own little colony. That gave them many advantages in Clichy, our poor Clichy. The children could learn to paint. They could read books, study music, enjoy the classics. Everything came naturally to them and if they wanted to learn Greek or Latin the family was not surprised. Whereas my situation was very different. I was a workman's son, and though learning, as such, was respected, there existed a very definite feeling that it was the hobby of the idle. One can hardly be surprised, can one, that in our youth, before the pendulum swung too far the other way, the workman found it hard to believe that reading a book was as hard as working ten hours with his hands?

'The pastor's family represented a code of morals that one was definitely aware of, and their church, surrounded by our miserable streets, shone in my youthful eyes like a castle. The Marogers, in short, were the squires of Clichy, good-looking, great-hearted, rich in learning, poor in money, and yet never ceasing to give to those poorer than themselves. The pastor was a Knight of the Round Table.'

He has become animated, more his real self, and I say:

'On the whole, it should be easier for a boy to succeed. With a boy it is merely a question of application.'

'Oh, it depends by what yardstick you measure success!' he exclaims. 'There are so many excellent scholars these days. One would need to be a Napoleon or a Pierre Curie! Individually I suppose we are all a trifle sentimental about our beginnings. All the same, I would like to write a history of Clichy, something along the lines of *L'Assommoir* of Émile Zola. I hope you would not accuse me of plagiarism?'

'Are you not in a position to defend yourself?' I ask, pointing to his many legal tomes.

He smiles and tells me that he is flying to Morocco later in the day to take part in some important case, and as we part he says:

'Let us meet again, shall we?'

The sun is very hot and I have a sudden desire to have my hair washed. Normally I wash it myself but I feel lazy, and as I am going to the theatre this evening, it would be nice to feel cool and fresh.

So here I am choosing a hairdresser at random and telling the girl I want a shampoo for long hair. How right I was to come here! This place is very pretty. There is a delicious smell of soap and water, and when I lean back in the chair and take the pins out my hair falls into a curved trough so that it can be washed behind me. This is delightful. I am immediately invigorated. This manner of leaning back to have one's hair washed is not popular in America and in England, and yet there is nothing quite like it for relaxing the muscles of face and neck, feeling expert fingers massaging the scalp—whereas to lift one's head soaking wet out of a basin, with one's face red and swollen, blood having rushed all the wrong way, as miserable as a poor dog thrown into a pond, what could be more uncomfortable? Besides, if it is merely a question of plunging one's head into a basin, one may as well do it at home and save the money!

When, having leaned back for ten minutes, my hair has been gently washed, I gather it up in a towel and cross over to the *salon*. One vast mirror covers the long wall. There are comfortable chairs, marble tables, no silly partitions. We are all in the same bright room and we can talk.

The hairdressers are extremely young men, and they wear white or sky blue jackets with short sleeves. The young man on my right is waving the old-fashioned way with tongs, and he stares at me with such insistence that I begin to feel shy: his colleague on my left is doing a permanent wave. My hair is dried carefully by hand, in a natural, healthy manner, and little by little it swells out into its full volume.

When the young man on my right has finished with his client, he comes over to me, and without a word of warning grasps my hair in the palms of both hands and shouts:

'I have never seen this before! It's neither dyed nor cut short! But you should not, you should not, allow your hair to grow like this. It must be agonizing to carry all this weight about with you. Cut it off! Cut it off!'

'No,' I answer firmly. 'The men in my family like my hair long, and one may as well be liked for something.'

'If you cut your hair,' he goes on, 'the men in your family might not even notice it, and you would be more comfortable. Besides, if you go on allowing it to grow like this, it will end by ageing you.'

'I do not agree,' I answer. 'However, I know exactly what is in your mind. If all women wore their hair long, there would be no work for the hairdresser.'

He laughs a young, honest laugh, amused to think that I should guess his stratagem. One of his colleagues calls out:

'We ought to add in our prayers: "May women never discover that long hair means bankruptcy for the hair-dresser!"'

My young man bends down and whispers:

'I'm not saying that it isn't attractive. I merely say that if you were my wife I should be in a perpetual state of agitation. My scissors would scream and give way to their nerves. They would want to snip, snip all the time.'

Then in a lower, more confidential voice:

'You must have a very sensual, vicious side to give life to all this hair, this living stuff, this savage, wonderful mane?'

At this I burst out laughing, and think of Ariane's father who, from the purity of his heart, from the austerity of his life, wants Ariane to keep her hair long. I laugh also because in a way I am delighted. Have I not always feared that men might think me rather old-fashioned, schoolmarmish, because I refuse to cut my hair? And now I am sensual and vicious!

'Stop laughing,' he says. 'I must put your hair up.'

Like a snake I hiss that he will not know how to put my hair up, that he is too young and inexperienced to put a real woman's hair up, and like a witch I cast a spell over him. He takes my hair in both hands, twists it, squeezes it, wrings it, bites his lips in annoyance and shame, loses his temper but cannot master it. Then, superb, I say to him: 'Look! It's easy!' and in less than a second I have folded my faithful hair, faithful to me alone, felt it spring obediently into place. Oh, happy is my lovely hair that I have allowed it to live, that I have forbidden that it should be massacred by cold, heartless scissors.

'Ah!' he says in frank admiration, 'I might have guessed that you alone could do it!'

With this I rise and depart, saluted by the hairdressers in turn, but feeling like a person who might have broken the bank at Monte Carlo, and knowing full well that they have but one hope—that I shall never come back.

In the rue Saint Dominique, on the left bank of the Seine, there is the Palace of Books where I am invited to watch the most celebrated authors autographing their works. This will amuse me. I shall be able to watch the agony of others with cruel eye.

There is a great crowd through which women with hats as wide as umbrellas pass with great agility. Teen-agers carry programmes on which they collect auto-graphs, not of authors, but of stage and film stars in the audience. The authors sit demurely at a long table behind the books they hope to sign, their names printed prominently above their celebrated heads as if they were rare orchids at a flower show. They look worried. I feel they would like to smile at us, to tempt us to buy; but they are writers, not salesmen, and must remain dignified. The audience is very elegant. Hélène Per-drière tells me about a visit to London. Next week she is off to Brussels. We are joined by Lycette Dar-sonval, famous dancer from the Paris Opera House. Our conversation takes a feminine turn. Here is General Maxime Weygand whose book *Recalled to Service* was recently published. Maurice Herzog, with his two children seated beside him, does his best in spite of frost-bitten hands to sign his book on the conquest of Annapurna. Mountains are very much in the news just now. A female author calls out to a bald gentleman: 'Good afternoon, general. Forgive me for not waiting to be spoken to, but at least you and I are of the same social world.' How royalist these

republicans are.   Only in Paris would you hear a thing
like that.   The Comtesse de Beaumont, who was once
anxious for my son to play in a French adaptation of
Henry James's *The Turn of the Screw*, is a writer as well as
an admirable hostess.   Her vivacity is such that I
wonder if her features are ever in repose.   My son
took to her immediately and it was then that I noticed
that he liked women to be elegant and lively.   I am
sorry in a way not to have allowed him to act in Paris.
It was that or an English private school.

Now I must leave these celebrities and get ready to
go to the theatre.

While Anita, the night chambermaid, runs my bath,
I find relaxation in cutting the pages of Mme Zézina's
book on telling one's fortune with playing-cards.

Anita has a tiny room at the very top of a large apartment house just off the Champs Élysées.   Thus she and
I both live on roof level at a short distance, as the sparrows
fly, from each other.   As she works at night, she has
to sleep during the day and this, she complains, is
difficult, particularly on Sundays, because the other
tenants of her roof-top insist on making such a noise.

'Now, madame, your bath is ready,' she says, 'and
while you have it I shall tidy up.'

'Anita, please don't throw any papers away, especially
paper that has wrapped up things, like lipstick and face
cream, that I have bought during the day.   I jot notes
down on everything.'

'I will do my best,' she sighs, 'but I simply have to
tidy up.   Tidiness is practically a vice with me.   When
I see odds and ends lying about, my fingers itch to
gather them up.   I assure you, madame, that when I go
to bed without putting something away, I can't sleep
till I have got up and put it away neatly.   Oh, you
would never find a blouse or a skirt lying about in my

room! Of course, in my profession, it's a great advantage. A chambermaid can never be too tidy.'

She now needs to remove the coverlet and fold back my sheets, but her eyes have fallen on the two packs of playing-cards that I have tumbled on my bed to work out some of the theories expounded in Mme Zézina's book, and she exclaims:

'Oh, madame, you can't leave all those playing-cards on your bed!'

'Do you believe in fortune-telling, Anita?'

'I have not had much experience with playing-cards,' she answers thoughtfully, 'but you have no idea of the things my sister could read in the palm of a hand. Honestly, the things she told us were uncanny. My father was the only one who absolutely refused to have his future told, but one day we girls badgered him so much that he exclaimed: "Very well. Just this once!" and no sooner had my sister taken his hand in her lap than she cried: "I know now why you were so secretive, dad. I can see police-officers and a jail—and all within a matter of weeks!" Father tried to be amused. He called us a pack of silly girls but he was worried all the same. In our small town in Switzerland the police and the local jail were not things to joke about, and father was a godfearing man. He was a shoemaker by trade, and as we girls worked as chambermaids in the hotels we used to persuade our guests to have their shoes repaired by him. The other hotel employees also sent him customers so that father, who used to work till midnight hammering and stitching in his shoemaker's shop, never taking more than a few hours to return a pair of shoes even if they had to be soled and heeled, made quite a lot of money. At the time this happened he had so much to do that he let out some of the rougher work to another shoemaker who had just set up business in a distant part of the town. Before

breakfast he went to the man's small workshop to
collect the shoes but he found it closed. "What an
hour of day to be still in bed!" thought father, and
started knocking the place down.   Then the neighbours
came out and said: "You're wasting your time.   The
police came to fetch him.   He must be in jail by now."
"In jail!" exclaimed father, "but that doesn't give me
back my shoes!   What will my customers say?"   Poor
father was in a great state and ran to the police-station
where, as the neighbours had said, the man was in jail.
Father had to go to the man's workshop between two
policemen to fetch his shoes.   You know what it is
with hotel guests.   They are here one day and gone
to-morrow, and if they send shoes to be mended they
must have them back quickly.   Imagine what father
felt like walking through the town with a policeman
on either side of him, and then he remembered how my
sister had seen it all in the lines of his hand.   But, of
course, father was not to blame.   The policemen were
simply coming along with the man's keys to open up
the workshop and give father back his shoes.   But it
does seem to prove, madame, that there is something
in fortune-telling, and that we women are more
perspicacious than men.'

'Indeed we are!' I cry.   'I have always thought it.'

Anita is full of wisdom.   She is perfectly happy in her
work, and tells me that politics bore her.

'But I really shouldn't say that,' she adds, 'because
the men must know what they are up to, putting up a
government and then knocking it down.   Paris is a
lovely place to live in.   Is there anywhere else in the
world where life is so agreeable?   The food, for instance, and the things one can do and see when one is
off?   Of course, one's work is much easier now than
when I was a girl.   You can't imagine what it was like
to work in provincial hotels, for instance, where there

was no running water, and where we used to have to
carry everything up and down six flights of stairs.
Work is a curious thing. I work because, quite frankly,
I like it. The tall girl who looks after you when I am
off works to put money in the bank. She even works
for the sake of earning a little more, when she is supposed to rest. Others work to buy what they see their
clients wearing. I don't think that's a bad idea. It's
lovely to feel that by work you can end by having what
you admire in other women. And now, madame,
go quickly and have your bath while I turn down the
sheets.'

Well, here I am back from my bath.

My dress is of dark blue foulard, and because of the
graceful curve of the pockets and the way it clings tightly
to my body, it looks like a closed umbrella. As my
dress was admirably fitted, the more I wear it, the more
I am in love with it. A dress signed by a great *couturier*,
that fits like a glove, immediately invests one with
enormous self-confidence.

When I wear my blue foulard dress I feel an important
person. If I see someone looking me up and down, I
whisper to myself: 'Maybe my dress does not please
that person who is looking me up and down, but nothing
will alter the fact that it is a dress by the great X, and
because it is by X nobody can possibly speak ill of it.'
So I no longer fear criticism. I am above the crowd.
My spirit is as light as air, and I actually feel beautiful,
for I know—yes, I know—that my dress is a masterpiece
made by the cleverest hands in the world. It is like a
man bearing in his arms a first folio of Shakespeare.
You cannot laugh at that man, for he carries a treasure
which invests his person with a halo.

Oh, how this lovely dress shows to advantage what is
good about my body! The girls who fitted me, kneeling

round me, pinching here, adding there, have reached the perfection of magicians in fairy-tales. I feel about this dress what I feel about truth in literature, that when, normally so unsure of myself as a writer, I have drawn the character of a living person, described some amazing but entirely true action, I have hoisted myself, because of the veracity of my facts, above the criticisms of the cruellest critics. A critic may say: 'This character is hateful. That action is base,' but he can never write: 'She is a liar. She writes nonsense,' for though her prose may be imperfect, it is invested with the halo of truth.

The Begum has sent her car, and, accompanied by her secretary, I arrive at a famous restaurant near the Odéon where the Begum and the Aga Khan are waiting for us. The Aga Khan looks tremendously happy and says he will not miss a single moment of the play, but the Begum, who has been attending fittings all the afternoon, swears she will not be hurried over dinner, and will throw her vows of slimming over the tree-tops of the Luxembourg.

We order a salad à la Niçoise, chops, fried potatoes, and strawberries and cream. Now, the Aga Khan infects us all with his gaiety. He is delighted to see his lovely wife breaking her diet and asks about her fittings. Without waiting for details of purely feminine interest, he asks:

'Are you pleased, my darling?'

'Delighted.'

'Then I am perfectly happy.'

We discuss a Nabob who has married the latest of a long line of wives, but to each he gives precisely the same jewels, for each wife has to give them back to him when she is divorced. The jewels have thus become rather like crown jewels to be handed from favourite to favourite. From this we go on to many strange tales about India. Suddenly the Aga Khan decides that he will go in advance to the theatre to be sure of getting there before the curtain rises. We watch him drive off in his car, and turn the corner to the Odéon. Ten minutes later the Begum, the English woman secretary, and I arrive in the darkened stalls. The curtain has already gone up. At the sight of us the Aga Khan breaks into loud laughter. We must have appeared to him like three female musketeers, though not of the same height, for I am small, the Begum tall, and the graceful secretary somewhere half-way between us. The audience is rather strait-laced, and later when I laugh too happily, the Aga Khan also, we both get dark looks. However, when the lights go on and the audience recognize the Aga Khan, who in Paris, as indeed everywhere, enjoys a great popularity, these same people surround him with great marks of affection, and at the end of the play escort him enthusiastically to the waiting car.

I smile without cynicism, enjoying this swift change in popular sentiment.

K

CHAPTER XVI

I HAVE HAD no time this morning for a new consultation, as I had planned, with Mme Zézina. Her book remains beside the playing-cards which Anita gathered up last night. Breakfast brought me a great many letters from London and page proofs of *Madeleine's Journal* which are to go back to-day. How expeditious we women are supposed to be. I suspect that men impose on us, but I shall be glad to hasten away these proofs before Anita comes to do her tidying.

Rain falls torrentially, and I have not seen a sparrow all the morning. Do they hate getting wet? What shall I wear, and with whom could I lunch? I am quite exhausted after my morning's work.

I have an idea. I shall lunch in the staff canteen. All the chambermaids tell me that the food is quite the best in Paris. I hurry down, delighted that I shall not be alone. There are a great many small tables, a crowd of laughing people, and the waiter whom everybody calls 'Rosette' because of his pink cheeks.

Rosette is adorable. I am joyously warned that he is tender and protective with women and has what the girls call the '*genre frôleur*,' that his hands gently graze our hair as he passes the dishes, and that he has a way of resting the tips of his fingers on feminine shoulders as he talks to us.

Well, at all events, here is spice to what might have been a lonely lunch.

'With me,' exclaims Rosette, defending himself, as he

faces our hilarious table, 'with me it's second nature.
I don't even know that I'm doing it.   But admit, ladies,
that an elegant shoulder would appear to be made
specially for a hand to rest upon it!'

'Naturally, Rosette!' I answer.   'I entirely agree.'

The people at my table introduce themselves.   There
is a girl telephonist, a young man from the reception
office, M. Grandjean, the hotel detective, and M. Émile
Boss, the *cantinier*, a fair-haired man of thirty-five, with
only one arm, who is in charge both of this canteen and
Christian Dior's on the other side of the Avenue Montaigne.   He is married, has a girl of twelve, and his
mother also works here.

The rain which just now I was deploring pleases the
cantinier because of his green peas.   His house just
outside Paris (it takes him three-quarters of an hour to
commute) has a fine kitchen garden in which he has
been sowing a vast quantity of green peas, and as soon
as they come up the birds eat them.   But there, he
loves the birds, and will not do anything to frighten
them away, so that he ends by wondering whether he
sows the peas for himself or for them.   He picked his
cherries on Sunday.   They were not quite ripe but if
he had waited another day—well, he likes the birds,
but they must not have everything!

A very young woman arrives late.   We are introduced,
but she exclaims:

'I know you very well, madame.   I am the deputy
supervisor of the floor on which you lodge, and it's my
business to see that the chambermaids do their work
properly.   I am very young, and it's nice to have such a
responsible job, but I do wish people were less untidy.'

'What!' I exclaim.   'You also?'

She laughs.

'I see you have been talking to Anita.   No, my
remark was not personal.   I think, on the contrary, you

are very good. You merely write notes on pieces of
paper. That is nothing. Some women who have
apartments next to yours seem unable to put anything
away—jewels, powder-boxes, money. One can easily
iron a dress and hang it up in a cupboard, but valuables
are such a nuisance. One ought to put them away, and
yet one hesitates to touch them. However, it is nice that
so many people make the top of the hotel their home.
They find it so much less trouble than running a house
with servants of their own. My ambition is to work
for a year in Spain. Spanish has become necessary.'

This desire to work in Spain blows across the girls of
Paris like a hot wind. I hear the same story everywhere. 'Oh, how we long to go to Spain!' When I
was a girl, most young people dreamed of London.
London was a city where one could make money easily,
working harder than the English, not hampered by
restrictions. To the West End hotels came real French-
men in the kitchens, real Italians as waiters. One ate
as one has forgotten to eat in the London of to-day, was
served as one is not likely to be served again. In Soho,
which reflected the picturesque side of this life, a street
market was busy till late at night, splashing the nocturnal
scene with vivid colour. Have we quite forgotten the
acetylene flares, the throb of a city's heart? Who will
make our hotels international again?

So, in Paris, every young woman is learning Spanish.
They all dream of spending their holidays in Spain.
Even a salesgirl at Christian Dior's said to me: 'What
makes a city agreeable to work in is to have some
money left over from one's wage-packet at the end of the
week. In Spain that is possible. Life is great fun but
not madly expensive. And there are servants to serve
even people like us. For after all, do we not all serve
somebody? What is this malady that makes certain
people revolt against serving? Do I not serve the

customer who comes to buy a dress at Christian Dior's? Then why should somebody be ashamed to serve me?'

What miracle is taking place in Spain?

Now Annie comes to join us, and Rosette brings us a bottle of red wine. Annie keeps the keys of the hotel show-cases in which the most famous firms in Paris display perfumes, hand-bags, scarves, shoes, lingerie, gold powder-boxes, and diamonds. Annie knows all the smart gossip, appreciates the beautiful things she sells, and speaks at least five languages perfectly. I am amazed how the most modest of the girls in the canteen speaks three languages with the perfection that denotes long spells abroad. Annie criticizes the too beautiful dogs brought in by wealthy clients. She exclaims: 'Keep your pedigree dogs, and give me a good mongrel!' Then seeing a copy of *France-Soir*, the evening paper, she turns avidly to our respective horoscopes.

One of the men starts to talk about his little family. He says that his children are almost bound, because of modern education, to be cleverer than he is. He is a floor-waiter born, I suspect, on a mountain slope.

'It has come to this,' he says almost comically. 'Men like myself, who are humble, must be content merely to breed. Our children are taken away from us and forcibly educated above our standard. We must consider ourselves lucky if they don't become ashamed of us.'

Suddenly his face lights up, and he says, turning to us, the women:

'I have a boy of sixteen. Of course, his mind is already running on the girls. His mother and I have noticed it for some time past, and as it was obvious he was courting one, we told him to bring her home. So he brought her to lunch on Sunday. A very nice girl, I must say, and in the evening at supper we told him so. "Oh, you know, dad," he said, "she's nice enough, but she's a long way from being worth a woman like mum. I don't suppose, between ourselves, that there are many like mum."'

How poignant this man's confession of pride that his son is not ashamed of his parents. He adds with beautiful simplicity:

'I, of course, personally think the world of my wife. But then I chose her. I married her. When I look into her eyes, I see her as she was twenty years ago. One hears so much about modern children saying heartless things, often on purpose to hurt, that to hear the lad speaking so affectionately, so respectfully, of his mother as if she were still pretty—as if I were a person who mattered—touched me deeply.'

He looks at us a little nervously, but we hide our emotion and find the word to make him laugh, to change the drama into comedy. Then Rosette arrives with a vanilla ice-cream as a present to me from the chef. The ice is delicious. We have coffee, the same as upstairs. We are all very gay. Then suddenly lunch-time is over. There is work to do.

I am invited by Monick and Gérard Boucheron to a cocktail-party at their very modern apartment overlooking the thickest, greenest part of the Bois de Boulogne. The apartment occupies the whole of a high-up floor with magnificent balconies, large rooms, wonderful cupboards and inventions, a dream kitchen, and servants' quarters adjacent to but sealed off from their own quarters—the sort of apartment that is too modern as yet to have made its appearance in the West End.

Cadillacs fill the private road between the tall white building and the Bois. I am late. Everything went wrong with my make-up, and there is a treacherous wind that is most disagreeable for one's hair.

I know in advance that I shall meet the great names of

the Paris luxury trades, names whose jewels, whose furs, whose perfumes, are known all over the world. Yes, and here is Jean-Jacques Guerlain coming out of his car to greet me.

Monick Boucheron looks like a flower on a long, thin stem, a Japanese poppy in a summer border that is agitated gracefully in a warm breeze. She has a lemon-coloured dress, and takes her duties of hostess seriously. A young mother, much in love, she is at the stage when the responsibilities of entertaining lie heavily on a head accustomed to pretty hats and gay laughter: her exuberance will be more in evidence when she goes to somebody else's party. Gérard, her husband, is tremendously gay. Soon there are so many people that one can scarcely move.

There is a rich buffet and champagne in abundance.

I am introduced to a young woman from the Lebanon about whom I already know something, for when I went to Deauville with Monick and Gérard in their car at Whitsun, I heard a good deal about her. She is small, has huge dark eyes, and in spite of the boisterous weather wears a bright red straw with a wide brim.

'I am so happy to be in Paris!' she exclaims, opening her dark saucers still wider. 'I spend hours visiting doctors and dressmakers. I am very lucky when I see only one doctor a day.'

She announces this with such life, with such tremendous fun, that I cannot believe there is anything seriously wrong, and when I tell her so she answers:

'Oh, but there is! Don't imagine that women who are always sighing, who always look as if they are beyond caring what happens to them, are necessarily less well than gay women, women who laugh all day like myself. I am glad also to have left the Lebanon. The Lebanon is a Garden of Eden, but as soon as one begins to fall ill there one must leave it. No climate is worse for asthma, sinus trouble, and low blood pressure. Personally I suffer the devil from all three! They make me miserably and chronically ill!'

She laughs delightfully, and goes on:

'If one has to be ill it is always more satisfactory to break a leg or fall over a precipice. Your friends rush to your bedside, and fill your room with flowers and sympathy, but tell them that you have merely asthma and sinus trouble! . . . Oh!' she exclaims. 'Look what a curious hat that woman is wearing! Do you like it?'

'No,' I answer, 'I do not.'

'Nor do I,' she says.

'Do you like Paris?' I ask.

'Enormously,' she answers, 'but it is always too hot or too cold. In Lebanon the seasons are more temperate. One knows when to expect the cold weather and when it will end. I understand now why you women in Europe have cupboards full of dresses which you show us saying: "I do so hope I shall have an opportunity to wear all these lovely things!" after which, during the whole season you go about in your tailor-mades with a white blouse! Of course, your tailor-mades are wonderful—the skirts and jackets mould your bodies as if they were sculptured on you. Personally I prefer light, gay dresses—dresses that I only wear once. We are not accustomed in our country to wear a dress more than once or twice, and never for more than a few hours at a time. I think we have fewer worries than you have—oh, of course, we have the same fear of death, but then death is inevitable, is it not? But women in my country have fewer everyday worries. For instance, just before leaving Lebanon I dreamed that my cook had gone off without finishing the strawberry syrup. As soon as I woke up, I ran to my mother and said: "I have just dreamed that my cook has left me." "Far from it," said my mother, "the good man is not leaving you. While you were dreaming about him, he made you twenty pots of strawberry syrup— but your dream is not altogether without foundation. Your brother's cook has just left him.'"

She goes on like some oriental singing bird:

'I myself am an excellent cook, for my mother taught me that a woman cannot successfully run a house unless she knows how to do perfectly all the things she asks her servants to do. I sought her advice, the other day, on how to prevent my cook from leaving me, and she said: "Work a little with him. Your kitchen is gay and full of sunshine, and as your cook will do the washing up, you will have nothing but the pleasure of cooking." A moment later she added thoughtfully: "Perhaps he would like you to buy him a machine for washing the dishes? That might encourage him to stay in your house."

'So I bought him a machine to wash the dishes, and all went well till he dropped the capsule of a mineral water bottle into the motor. "Very well," I said, "as you are so clumsy with machinery, you will revert to washing up by hand." "That will be quite all right," he answered happily. "I shall tell the other cooks that I found the machine unsatisfactory. I shall say it did the washing up much less well than I do it myself."'

She leaves me to join another woman whom she has recognized in the crowd, and I watch her red straw hat waving like a poppy in a cornfield. Soon her laughter dominates the noise. In truth, she exhales the perfume of the early French novels about the Lebanon in which the châtelaine, living in a white colonial house, was served by a great number of 'boys,' and I can imagine her, with a sun-helmet and a hunting-crop, going out with a good-looking young officer.

Two women beside me are talking in a low voice, and I find myself intently listening.

'My dear,' says one, 'a four hours' fitting to-morrow. It makes me ill to think of. What a lot of trouble we women do give ourselves in order to be unfaithful to our husbands. One ought to dance naked at the Folies Bergères. Those women have all the luck.'

'Oh no,' answers her companion. 'From mother to daughter, for generations, the women in my family have been brought up on fittings and social calls, and if it were my profession to show myself naked on the stage, I would be bored to death. Besides, I would quickly be tired of the sight of my body.'

A man joins them. He appears gay and witty, and as he saw them from afar talking in low tones, he guessed that the conversation was about dresses and love. He discusses fashion with sense and experience, and exclaims suddenly:

'I simply love talking about women!'

That makes them both laugh.

A man alone in a corner of the room smiles at me. He comes over and says:

'I really don't know what I am doing here. All this noise! All these people! My whole mind is centred on little children. I am acquainted with this family because two years ago, while the parents were abroad on business, their little boy was brought to me dying, and we were just in time to save him. My domain is the Children's Hospital, and I simply do not exist outside it, though there is often more sadness than joy. Telephone me one morning before nine, and I will show you some children who will interest you. You are a woman writer, are you not? That is a good thing for a woman to be if she is sensitive. Now I must be going. There is too much noise. It drives me mad.'

I am introduced to an American who speaks admirable French. He pays me a very pretty compliment, and I answer:

'I am inclined to think that Frenchwomen, on the whole, are less beautiful than the American women I meet in New York.'

'I agree,' he says, 'but there is no place in the world where women are so well turned out as in Paris. With the aid of artifice their very defects become their most striking features.'

'These cocktail-parties do not show us at our best,' I say. 'I love them. They are very amusing. One meets a great many people, but one steps out of a tiny French elevator into a crowded room. What would the women one reads about in nineteenth-century novels say, who were always complaining of having their dresses crushed by having to be seated too long on their At Home days. I think we must at least be stronger physically to remain standing for so many hours on high heels. Historians pity the Chinese women who had their feet bound. I doubt if they suffered as much—but of course, we love it.'

'I suppose you do,' he says.

I decide to leave, and as it has started to rain, and I cannot find a cab, I ask a very elegant young couple to take me as far as the Champs Élysées. They accept but with bad grace. I soon discover that this has nothing to do with me, for as soon as we are in the car I realize that I have intruded on a quarrel—a quarrel between young people born into the top drawer of French society, who have acquired by environment and education so perfect a command of the French language, that without the slightest inflexion, without departing from the most perfect good manners, they can deeply wound each other, drawing blood, with phrases barbed with poison.

She is hard and magnificent: he is cold and aristocratically good-looking. Only in Latin countries does one still meet these cruelly supercilious young sons of wealthy families. I cannot discover the cause of the quarrel. Occasionally it appears to me of the highest gravity: at other times disconcertingly childish; but seeing a cab rank, I ask to be dropped at the top of the line. They oblige with cold courtesy, and I feel that as soon as they have got rid of me, their quarrel, which smouldered in my presence, will have a chance to flare up and consume itself.

I am to dine with friends at Claridges, and as I enter this magnificent hotel, I am reminded that it was here that my mother and I came to meet the man who brought me as a girl to England for the first time. I am glad to discover that my girlish eyes did not exaggerate the beauties of this hotel, which is indeed full of old-fashioned grace. My girlhood impressions were, I find on revisiting so many scenes of past events, more accurate than I dared to believe.

These high-ceilinged public rooms with tall, gentle mirrors throw one back into a period when war had not demolished so many lovely cities, when there was no Iron Curtain, and when one could leave it casually to the porter to reserve a sleeping-berth for Berlin, Warsaw, Budapest, or Bucharest.

How pleasant it is to dream. Perhaps it is one of the charms of being a sensitive woman.

CHAPTER XVII

THIS INVITATION to a wedding has followed me from London to Normandy, and from Normandy to Paris—and now suddenly I notice that it is for to-day.

Thérèse, my cousin Rolande's daughter, is to be married this morning in the Valley of Chevreuse. The story of her family, my family, leaps to my mind. My mother and I are all that are left on her mother's side. I must attend this wedding. I ask the waiter who has brought my breakfast how to reach the place named on the card. He says I must take the subway to Denfert-Rochereau where I shall find an electric train. There will be no work this morning. My mail shall remain unanswered. I do my hair, I dress, and at nine I leave the hotel.

I have not been out so early since I went to market, and I am almost surprised at the crowds in the subway train which, as it emerges from the tunnel under the Seine, throws into sudden relief the tremendous base of the Eiffel Tower whose summit is enveloped in thick mist. Next to me a young man, though it is only nine-fifteen, is reading this morning's *Daily Express*.

My troubles start at Denfert-Rochereau. I take a train going in the right direction but I forget to change, with the result that I reach a most delightful spot called Fontenay-aux-Roses. The place is well named. Roses abound, fall over each other in massed garlands all over the station. I am convinced that I shall easily find a car to take me across country to my destination, but when I

149

ask two employees mending a gate to direct me to the nearest garage, one of them exclaims:

'But my poor little lady, you'll never find an automobile here. This is a village where rich city folk own week-end villas. By Tuesdays the place is deserted. There's nothing left but us and the roses. Wait for the next up train, which will take you back to the station where you should have got out. You are lucky there is one. At least you will be in time for the wedding breakfast!'

This station is really adorable. What I like is the old-fashioned simplicity of these roses. They are of the kind that creep round the doorways of thatched cottages in old, unspoilt villages. The morning air is warm and sweet.

A little woman arrives with a black poodle bitch straining on the leash like an angry sheep. The woman tells me that it is because she has to muzzle her for the train journey.

'If I conform to the regulations,' she says, 'she can travel in my compartment. Of course, as soon as I am in the train I take her muzzle off.'

We have ten minutes to wait, and as we are two women alone we start to gossip. She is no longer young, and like all the women of her age in France, she has dyed her hair. Hairdressers must make a great deal of money dyeing hair, for no woman would allow herself to be seen at work with grey hair. She lives at Bourg-la-Reine and travels every morning to Orsay, which is the station where I ought to have got out. She is short and fat, laughs all the time, and her eyes dart about her taking everything in. After a while her eyes rest on me.

'So you forgot to get out of the train?' she says, looking at me curiously. 'It's such an easy journey. How could you make a mistake? I do it every day.'

'It is doubtless because you do it every day,' I answer,

'that you think it is so simple. I know I'm rather a silly woman, but I am delighted to be in a position to make mistakes in the train. I would hate to have to go to the same place every day. I have never been any good at doing the small things in life, and I quite understand Sacha Guitry saying that he is frightened of buses and subways.'

The poodle has put her paws on my skirt and appears to want something.

'Ah!' says the woman. 'Dogs are very intelligent, especially bitches. Fifille is asking you to take her muzzle off. As she knows that it was I who put it on, she has no hope that I will take it off yet—whereas, thinks Fifille, you might possibly take pity on her. No, really, I would not be without a dog. I could not bring myself to give up the chance of being loved so faithfully. A dog loves you even when it is asleep. But please do not think that I am one of those selfish women who prefer dogs to people. Not a bit of it. I have a grown son who is married, and I am already a grandmother. So you see that I am in a position to judge people as well as animals, but dogs go on loving you longer than children. And one is not in a continual state of alarm about their health, as one is with a child.

'I work very hard but I enjoy myself enormously. I am a cinema attendant in the little town to which we are going, and every morning, in sunshine, rain, sleet, or snow, my dog Fifille and I walk four or five miles across country. That is why you see us at this station. We have walked from home.

'I spend so much time in the dark, you understand? I am at the cinema till nearly midnight, showing people to their seats. I would have a face the colour of a turnip if I did not take plenty of fresh air in the morning.

'The wonderful thing is that I am never tired of watching the films they put on at the picture house. I must even confess to you that on the days when they change the programme I arrive quite excitedly, a few minutes early. I simply can't help it. I am like a child. On those mornings nobody is better pleased to get to work than I am.

'Some film stars I love: others I detest. I cannot tell you what it's like to spend entire days looking at the face of a person you can't stand. It's all very well to tell me that I am not obliged to look. Well, I just have to look. I don't think I would mind so much if I could tell the patrons how I hated certain stars, but if I did that they might keep away from the picture and where would my tips be? There's one French girl, for instance, who rubs me up the wrong way the moment I see her silly face on the screen. I could kill her. Then there's the young man who thinks he is so beautiful. One feels certain he must spend his entire week-ends measuring his chest and his biceps. Oh, these blond male beauties with their silly blue eyes! They positively revolt me. I would put them all in a tumbril and send them to the guillotine.'

'Which are the ones you like?'

A delightful tenderness transforms her features. The American men are very virile. She is perfectly crazy about some of them. There is also Serge Reggiani. What a man! Amongst the women, Danielle Darrieux, Viviane Romance, Michèle Morgan. . . .

'One ends by learning all about the film industry,' she says, laughing. 'It took me a little time not to mind the interruptions, the people who keep on arriving and who need to be taken to the right-priced seats. Ours is a continuous performance, did I tell you? However, it's amazing how one gets not to notice the patrons. One takes them automatically to their seats, and all the time one's eyes are watching the screen. Then, of course, if one does miss anything important, one has plenty of opportunities to see it again, and when, on Saturday nights, the house is full, the usherettes have a right to sit down at the back.

'No, really. I would not change my job for anything. Luckily the picture theatres have trouble in finding good usherettes. We have to be very strong in the legs, and have a way with patrons. Some of them need watching.'

She looks at me archly, and adds:

'I wouldn't mind betting you don't mind being kissed in the dark yourself?'

Now we are in the train Fifille no longer has her muzzle, and the little woman, like a faded leading lady in a provincial touring company, continues untiringly to talk.

'I make a lot of money,' she exclaims. 'I have bought a pretty cottage further up in the Valley of Chevreuse, and my husband and I go there when we have a day off. It's such a darling cottage that we improve and beautify it for our old age.'

'I suppose,' I ask, 'your husband is also in the motion picture business?'

'Heavens, no!' she exclaims. 'My husband is a "tough" one. He drives a milk truck. Yes, he's as hard as hard. Every night I hurry home, and if I am on time we have a quarter of an hour together. He leaves at twelve-fifteen to the second so if I am late we miss each other. His job is thunder and lightning: it's no job for half a man. A man to drive a truck like that has to be one hundred per cent a man. Consider that at ten-thirty this morning he was not yet home. That means over ten hours at the wheel, half the time probably in a thick mist.

L

'But he has seven days off all at once during which to
right his nerves.   Then he comes to fetch me every
evening at the cinema—and I try to get away early.

'Yes, really, I have a fine husband, and it's nearly
twenty-five years that we've been married.'   She beams.
'A husband, a dog, and a rare amount of money to
spend!   My boy's marriage is the only thing that worries
me at all—she is eighteen, pretty in a Simone Simon
way, but so untidy!   When their love for each other
cools off, I feel that things may not be easy.

'I do so hope they don't divorce.   I think it is wrong
to divorce when there are children.   For instance,
madame, did you read about that boy of twelve whose
stepfather did not love him?   And then his mother, to
please her new husband, beat him.   He hanged himself
in the kitchen just as he had seen it done in a film.
Oh, madame, I cried so.'

The little woman has made me so interested in her
life that I am glad now that I made a mistake about the
trains.   I feel that whatever happens, everything is going
to be for the best—that time and place do not matter.

At Orsay we discover a mechanic working under the
chassis of a motor-car, and Fifille, who apparently
knows the mechanic, takes advantage of his recumbent
position to lick his face all over.   Urged by my companion to help me, the mechanic rises, wipes his hands
on an oily rag, and agrees to drive me to Briis.   So I
take farewell of the usherette and her poodle.

How lovely is the Valley of Chevreuse!

Though we are comparatively near Paris, the country
has all the charm of French peasant land.   We skirt
magnificent estates and vast farms, and cornfields are
filled with the scarlet poppy.

Now here is the church spire of Briis-sous-Forge.
Midday is striking, and I have certainly missed the

wedding. My sudden fear, as I have warned nobody of my coming, is that the family and guests will have dispersed or gone off to another village.

We reach a baker's shop. This bakery belongs to Paul, the husband of Rolande, my little cousin, who died at the beginning of the war from the illness for which she went to the sanatorium at Groslay. The bakery is closed, and a woman, dressed entirely in black except for white gloves, exclaims as I try the door:

'Madame, you cannot buy any bread to-day. The baker is at his daughter's wedding.'

'I have come from Paris to attend the wedding, madame,' I answer.

The old lady looks me up and down. My coat and skirt, though made in Savile Row, do not come up to her idea of what is required for a village wedding in France. I feel that I am not making a good impression, but after a moment she says:

'A *vin d'honneur* is being held in the inn.'

My driver turns perilously in the narrow road, and soon we are in front of the inn. Ah! Here are the dresses of the women guests—those azure blues, those pinks so favoured by elegant young ladies in French villages.

I climb oak stairs, very old and picturesque, and I reach a long, low room with trestle-tables covered with beautiful white cloths—and at the far end of one of the tables I see my little bride, who looks like a girl in a communion dress. She looks up, and is so overcome with surprise at my presence that she utters a cry and bursts into tears—and I am so moved to see her in her wedding dress that I start to weep myself.

She is the picture of my poor Aunt Marie-Thérèse, and of my aunt's daughter Rolande. She is both of them, but as fresh as a rose, her eyes limpidly blue, one slightly smaller than the other. Do you remember how

Marie-Thérèse also had this singularity due, she used to say, to having been left out all night in the forest of Russy at Blois by my forgetful grandmother?

'Oh!' exclaims Thérèse, wiping her tears, 'how happy I am that you should have come, my dear Madeleine! I was so sad to have nobody from my own family. How happy I am! Here is my husband. He is a pastry-cook and his name is André.'

She blushes and adds:

'Do I say things very stupidly? I am so excited and agitated, and yet I didn't cry once during the church service. It was only when I caught sight of you that I cried.'

I look with interest at Paul, the baker-pastry-cook, who married Rolande, almost a sister to me, after my departure for England. Rolande was desperately in love with him. He had been her one great love. He is now rather fat, but, after all, he was always massive. My mother and I thought it surprising that a girl as slight, as elfish, as Rolande should choose a man physically so different, but it was his strength, of course, that she admired in him, his energy and splendid good health.

This is how they had met.

After the death of my Aunt Marie-Thérèse, my Uncle Louis gave up their apartment in the rue de Longchamp, took Rolande out of the sanatorium at Groslay, and made a new home for her in a pretty suburb near Versailles. Rolande used to buy the bread every morning at a fine bakery where a tall, strong, young man turned his dark eyes with interest upon her. She thought him irresistible as he emerged in his white linen trousers from the bakery, bringing up the long, crisp, hot loaves in wicker baskets. He was gay and smiled at her. She was fascinated by his powerful muscles and the hair on his chest powdered with flour. He could not believe that any girl could be so appealingly delicate. They looked out eagerly for each other. The daily bread, for Rolande, became the symbol of hope, better health, love—and life itself. Her love was not merely great and beautiful, but coming, in her case, from a body undermined by her cruel illness, it achieved unusual proportions. Her heart at least was young and vigorous.

They were married, and when we heard that Rolande was expecting a baby, we feared it might kill her, but no, she had a little girl whom they called Thérèse after my gay and pretty aunt.

Rolande was not allowed to keep her child. For four years the baby girl had to remain away from her mother in a completely safe environment. Paul's love for his young wife kept her alive, and then came the joyful moment when, just before the Second World War, they were all together. Rolande came to stay with me in Normandy, and I marvelled at the way she sewed her lingerie with needles that one could hardly see. I thought she had become slighter, more ethereal, than I had ever known her. The slightest thing exhausted her but she was happy.

Then war came. Paul went off to be a cook in a hospital train, and Rolande, robbed of the presence of her robust husband who was always so gay and affectionate, felt less well. The Germans turned the Maginot Line. There followed Dunkirk, the fifth columnists, the refugees, and the dive-bombing.

Rolande's illness, which since her marriage had appeared quiescent, broke into swift flame. There was no news of Paul. The neighbours were packing to flee. My Uncle Louis stayed with her. She made tremendous efforts to be brave. She even made some light dresses— we all start to sew in moments of extreme emotion— and Rolande said to Louis: 'It is May and when Paul comes on leave I want him to see me looking pretty.'

She said she would go to the hairdresser because Paul loved her hair, but though she was desperately tired she explained: 'It's only a phase, and will pass. I have known worse. If only Paul would come I would soon feel better.'

My Uncle Louis brought her lunch in on a tray: then went back to the kitchen for some cherries, the first of the year. He spoilt his daughter as he had spoilt her mother. He was put into the world to spoil women, women who were ill and needed him. If there were cherries in the shops, Rolande must have some. He came back to her, calling:

'Cherries, my darling! The very first of the year!'

But she was dead, and all round the little house refugees were starting on the great trek.

My mother and I received a telegram in Normandy. We hesitated whether to go. Thank God we did not, for we might not have returned alive. A few hours later we were ourselves fleeing to Saint-Malo.

Thérèse was not quite ten. She had been sent away a second time. Paul was neither killed nor taken prisoner, and some years later he married again, a young woman called Antoinette who loved Thérèse as dearly as the two sons she quickly gave Paul.

Antoinette is here. I am introduced.

I also make friends with the two little boys, one of whom is angry because his big sister is leaving home. The local chemist is, it appears, a little hurt because he would like to be placed beside the veterinary surgeon's wife who is young and pretty, but that seat is already engaged. It was at this point that I arrived, and going straight up to Thérèse was made guest of honour, even taking precedence over the wife of the mayor. Paul tells me all this, employing for the first time with me the affectionate 'thee' and 'thou.'

The bride and bridegroom lead the way down, and

are photographed in front of the inn, after which we—
the family—go to the bakery. There are great ogival
doors which Paul opens with an old-fashioned iron key,
then out comes a spaniel who puts his cold nose into my
hand. He was alone in the house, guarding it.

There is a wonderful garden with a vine-covered
south wall (the back of the hairdresser's house): roses
and apple-trees smell sweet, and now we pass into a
tiled room with an immense refrigerator in which Paul
had put his daughter's wedding cake. A passage
leads to the ovens, which are still warm though there is
no baking to-day.

Paul shows me the kneading machine. There is
pride in his voice as he says, placing a hand lovingly
against the side: 'Forty years old. Our generation.
Listen how the echo rings clear and true.' He knocks
it lightly with two fingers. 'Listen!' he repeats.

What is pretty also is the device whereby the flour
comes down through the ceiling from the attic where it
is stored. None must be spilled, for, says Paul,
'flour is the baker's big expense, and if he wastes it
he will not grow rich.' The long peels are so smooth
that, as they stand against the wall, they look like the
narrow tongues of prehistoric animals. Hanging from
old beams are the bread baskets shaped like babies'
cots, rows of them.

The cake moulds are of every shape, and I would like
to know all about them, but a master baker, son of a
master baker whose family has baked for generations, is
not patient with women who ask questions. He says,
like my little woman at the station at Fontenay-aux-
Roses, when she talked about trains: 'It is so easy. I
do it every day.' Of course, Paul finds it no trouble to
make bread and cakes. He makes them every day. It
is as easy for him to make them as it is for us to eat them.

We go into the shop.

Antoinette has dressed the windows with dolls in white communion dresses, for last Sunday was set aside for first communions, and next Sunday will be the same, so the dolls will remain in the windows till then. 'Afterwards,' says Antoinette, 'we shall put the little dolls to sleep again till next year.'

How good the shop smells. There are long narrow strawberry and cherry tarts, the fruit ripe and juicy, the pastry made with fresh butter, and apple and apricot flans.

The mother of the bridegroom is rather frightening: her huge hands are those of a woman who has done an enormous amount of work, who has washed mountains of sheets. A tiny ring, a girl's ring, is on a very rugged finger. Paul says to me: 'She has property tucked away, and as André, her son, is an only child, the young people will be well off.'

'Yes,' I think. 'Anybody can see that this big woman has a bit of land, something in the bank—what the provincial French call so picturesquely: *'du répondant,'* something to answer for their reputations!' She is to pay half the expenses of the wedding, and I take her to be pious.

She calls for a bottle of champagne, a box of *petits fours*, and a big vanilla ice, the sort that pastry-cooks in France make for a family. Antoinette goes to the refrigerator, brings these things out, and does them up in paper and string. André's mother picks up the ice and the biscuits, but finding them awkward to carry, exclaims in a voice that is strangely plaintive for a woman who looks so much like a man:

'Will not somebody help me to carry these things?'

As I feel a little chilly in this closed baker's shop, and as I am very intrigued by the old lady's request, I ask her if I may carry the champagne. Thus we go out together into the street.

Soon we are walking silently side by side through the

village, she very tall, with manly stride, I very small, perched on high heels. In front of us is the lovely medieval church. Ah! I have suddenly understood! We are going to offer a share of the wedding feast to the *curé*, who this morning married our two children. How perfectly charming!

At the side of the presbytery a door with a judas stands ajar. We ring. A bell jingles out, but without waiting for anybody to appear we enter.

I cannot believe that I am not dreaming, for we have suddenly entered a real presbytery garden—yes, just like those presbytery gardens I have so often read about in French novels—moss-roses, old-fashioned red roses that fill the air with pungent smell, gooseberry bushes, lettuces, birds gorging everywhere on fruit ripening in hot sunshine.

A priest appears on the threshold of the presbytery. He is most put out, he says, holding a white linen napkin in front of his mouth. He has just broken two teeth, or at least he thinks he has broken two, but he might just as well have broken three—or perhaps only one. He invites us to follow him into the dining-room where his vicar, *Monsieur le Curé-Doyen*, is seated at table having lunch with two very old servants, wearing different but strange apparel. One has the top of her head wound about with a tall black bonnet, the other is less old, but appallingly ugly.

The *curé-doyen* and the two servants rise. They would appear to have stepped out of eighteenth-century memoirs. One would expect a diligence to clatter through the village, or to meet a nobleman in a powdered wig. A great many compliments are spoken in extremely choice French. Enchanting things are said about the bride. Finally the *curé-doyen* asks me in the most polite way whence I have sprung, and when I tell him that I have come from England he says:

'Ah, madame, ever since I saw the coronation of your beautiful young queen on television, with that historic and deeply impressive religious ceremony in the abbey where William the Conquerer was crowned, I have for England, madame, a new and deeper respect. When, the next day, I celebrated mass in our village church, I felt very small before God.'

André's mother and I stand before him, looking strange, holding our gifts in front of us.

The *curé-doyen* is full of fun. He has not lost his teeth, and his eyes are now turned towards the bottle of champagne that I am nursing like a doll, and he appears to be saying that he will do honour to this great wine. He is the doyen of all the priests in this part of the Seine-et-Oise, and he comes to lend a hand on special occasions, for there is, alas, a great shortage of priests in France, and many beautiful churches are locked on Sundays, for there is nobody to say mass. The bright and pretty presbytery was once an adorable school run by nuns, but it was obliged to close when the parents took their children away to send them to the State school.

André's mother and I now return to the inn where the wedding breakfast is taking place. Every time the door opens and the fat, pink-cheeked servant-girl arrives with a new and succulent dish, she is clapped and cheered. My little bride, for whom I have a growing affection, has moved a vase of arum lilies from in front of her to see me more easily, and I am happy to read in her eyes how tenderly, while looking at me, she thinks of her mother, for to-day is the thirteenth anniversary of Rolande's death. And in my ears echoes the din of the great exodus.

CHAPTER XVIII

AT NINE I am in the hall waiting for Dr Hofmann, who has offered to take me with him to two of the hospitals where he works. We drive immediately to the 'red' belt which encircles Paris: the tall, grey, leprous houses are not pretty to look at in the rain. Here and there rise great new apartment houses for those who, in my girlhood, were known as the working classes.

Dr Hofmann is in love with Paris. He likes the wide avenues and quiet leafy squares of the rich and noble districts as much as these drab grey houses which grew up like fungus against the old city walls. All the conflicting pictures of Paris, rich, poor, old, or new, spell joy to this son of a village shopkeeper in the Dordogne, who since the first day of his arrival, fired with a determination to study medicine, has crossed and recrossed the bridges of the Seine so often that there is not a single corner of his beloved city that he cannot see clearly, he says, merely by closing his eyes.

His chief, he continues, talking of the famous specialist under whom he studied as a young man, was a typical professor of the old school.

'These men,' he muses, 'were both doctors and actors. My chief, for instance, would never enter hospital without ceremoniously removing his hat as a sign of respect to the busts of all the celebrated doctors lined up in the hall on marble pedestals, and he would insist that now and again we should stand in front of them to observe a minute's silence.

'At the start of each lecture, he would harangue us more or less in these words:

'"Medicine," he would say, "is a vocation. If money is what you are after, you would do better to become a grocer or a haberdasher. I have left the door of the lecture room wide open. Let those who wish go out!"

'Not one of us ever moved. He would then walk very solemnly to the door and close it, after which the lecture would begin.

'He had an uncanny gift of sizing up his pupils. We started by being about a hundred strong but he quickly made up his mind that only thirty showed promise. He advised the others to marry rich women and buy themselves chemists' shops.

'After a year or two, he narrowed the thirty down to three. These, he decided, must continue at all costs. I am proud to say that I was one of them, but in fact, deep within me, I had no need of this affirmation of what I already knew with such certainty. The sacred flame burned in my heart. I asked him once if he had been a brilliant student himself. His dark eyes deepened, and he answered:

'"At school I was not at all extraordinary. I held myself back like a racehorse. Then when it came to studying medicine I let myself go, and I passed out top of the list with marks that have never been equalled since. Second to me was my very eminent colleague, Professor Gosset, now known all over the world."

'Our chief was so brutally outspoken that his sort of language would no longer be tolerated. It came, I think, from a general feeling among doctors, so aware of how little they knew, that if they shouted loud enough they would appear to know more than they did. A man often raises his voice to cover up a weakness.

'Nevertheless I venerate his memory because behind the stage effects there were the mind and soul of a great and good man. Teaching methods have radically changed in a lifetime. Violence, in speech or manner, is outmoded in the individual. Yes, of course, it was a defect, though a lovable one, to take terribly to heart what one worshipped, one's God, one's country, one's profession. Men have lost the virile reflex. The man who is insulted, who hears his wife insulted, pretends he has not heard. He no longer responds to the primordial temptation to punch the other fellow on the nose. We saw that here during the German occupation. Instead of scratching out the eyes of the invader, like the angry cock on our national emblem, we found excuses for it all. Radio, television, and the films have also a bad influence in this respect. We become less patriotic, seeing too easily, in broadcasts and pictures, the qualities of other nations. But this is politics. Just allow me to say that we are all reasonable, much too reasonable.'

Here is Villejuif.

The hospital is immense: part of it is reserved for the aged, and I suddenly recall that Mme Maurer used to visit the cemetery once a month because her husband, who died in the hospital, was buried here.

Little old men and little old women trot along in twos. One old lady has a fashionable hat with a veil.

'Yes, indeed,' says Dr Hofmann as he parks the car behind others in the yard, 'the old ladies are very coquettish. They even marry, and there are abominable scenes of jealousy. We spoil them. They have theatrical and film shows.

'The old people have no business to be here. They should go to a home in the country. We lose a few but new ones continually come. And yet if you only knew how we need the beds! Alas, it's all politics. They have voted Communist. They are keen Socialists. The municipalities have therefore an interest in keeping them in town.'

We now enter the hospital: two doctors with lamps attached to their foreheads are examining a patient. 'Now, Madame Henrey,' says Dr Hofmann, 'take off your jacket. Mme Thorez will give you a white overall so that you can stay with me.' Two nurses, very young, bare-legged but with rather high heels, are sterilizing instruments. A young woman arrives and is asked to sit down. She describes her symptoms. A doctor asks gravely but with just enough gaiety to take away her nervousness:

'You haven't vomited, madame?'

'No, doctor.'

'Good, and what about those little ulcers in the mouth. Do you often have them?'

'I had pleurisy a few years ago, doctor.'

'Do you get tired easily, madame?'

Mme Thorez is standing beside the doctor, taking everything down on a sheet of paper. She bends over the patient and gently asks her to spell out the name and address.

Dr Hofmann appears in white: he even has a big white apron round his waist, and now Mme Thorez helps me to put on a coat that smells of linen freshly boiled and which buttons up on the man's side. I am completely transformed. Dr Hofmann and two other doctors are looking at the results of an X-ray. They look first at one photograph, then at another, and I hear him say: 'We shall have to operate, make an incision here. There's nothing else we can do. I am going to take Mme Henrey round a moment. I'll be back later.'

We look in at the 'amphi' as Dr Hofmann calls it. A professor is drawing on a blackboard with red and white chalks. I become instantly keyed up. He is talking about a hospital case of vaginitis in a girl of six. The organs are so recognizably drawn that I realize with some surprise that the diagram might be that of an adult woman instead of a child. There follow learned explanations which I cannot understand, but the students, many men and just a few women, listen intently.

More out-patients: two little girls asleep, the head of one resting on a shoulder of the other. One remembers children sleeping thus along the roads of France during the great exodus, children sleeping from exhaustion while parents frantically bought petrol to continue the mad flight . . . evacuees also from London after the first raids, children sleeping pitifully, shoulder against shoulder, in damp shelters, children accustomed to seeing abnormal things happening round them. Are these accustomed to sadness and disease? The doctor bends over them: one little girl opens her eyes and smiles. 'Head tumours,' he whispers. 'That is why they assume the pose of sleepers. They are not asleep.'

Women knit, men do crossword puzzles, and about the great hall stalks fear: faces that look up at us smile because of our white blouses; and I am choked with emotion.

'Over here,' says Dr Hofmann, 'is the cancer research wing.'

The two doctors we left behind are discussing a fresh lot of X-ray photographs. One of them turns quickly to Dr Hofmann and says:

'We have an appointment at the Pitié. Should we not go?'

'Yes,' Dr Hofmann answers, taking off his blouse. 'Let us go.'

The Pitié is vast, modern, not ugly at all because each wing is divided from the other by beautiful gardens and tall, leafy trees. Near us is the magnificent Salpétrière where Dr Axel Munthe spent those memorable hours with Dr Charcot which he describes in *San Michele*.

Cautiously I ask my two companions if they have

read *San Michele*.   Dr Hofmann read it rather a long time ago but says he liked it, and will reread it.   His companion was chiefly impressed by Dr Munthe's success in the social world.   Well, at any rate, both men have read the book.   That is what matters for an author, and I remember the president of E. P. Dutton in New York telling me that they had so little belief in its success that they only published a few hundred copies.   Somebody rang up from Brooklyn one day and asked: 'Say mister, have you read this book you've just published?'

I would not have thought about this if I had not seen the Salpétrière looming in front of me.   I am reminded of an eighteenth-century print of Paris with all these trees, the sort of print one buys on the quays.   Paris remains the Paris of the Bourbon kings, and it is curious that the French capital, which is republican, changes so little compared with London, which one would expect to be conservative because of the monarchy.

'Come and see my patient,' says Dr Hofmann.

A men's ward.

One man lies facing the wall as if he were already dead. Others appear to look right through us, eyes glazed. The doctor's patient, his neck heavily bandaged, is sitting up in bed. · He speaks in the tiniest, thinnest voice, a voice without volume.   His hands are those of a labourer, and I reflect that he is the sort of man who, in my youth, would probably have shaved twice a week and only worn a collar on Sundays.   He shakes hands with Dr Hofmann, who takes the bandages off, exposing the wound.

'Splendid,' says the doctor.   'To-morrow you will be back with your family, and you can come and see me every day at the Villejuif.   It's nice to talk again, isn't it?   Good-bye, my friend.'

I also bid the man good-bye, but I can scarcely stand. My legs double up under me.   My forehead is damp.

'I'm really pleased with that man,' says Dr Hofmann. 'Think of it—only five days since he was operated on for cancer of the throat, and he has his voice back already. I am going to send him home, to be with his family, because here he sees men die all round him, and in the end he might take it badly. The other doctors blame me, but I know I am right.

'Surgery is wonderful, but the glory should go to the nurses. We have the honours: they have the sadness, the loathsome dressings, the terrifying contacts. Without the nurses we could do nothing. Have you ever thought of nights in a ward like this?

'There are times when, as I walk through the cancer wards, I try to escape the eyes of the poor devils who stare at us. One feels so terrible to have done all one can for them, not to be able to do anything more. Some of them know it. They hate us for being so ignorant. This horrible thing is immense, beyond us for the moment.'

We meet his colleague.

'How's your patient?' Dr Hofmann asks.

'Not too bad, but I got no sleep on account of him. I shall try to take a fortnight's holiday now. I was thinking about San Remo.'

We drive back to the heart of the city, and Dr Hofmann tells me about his son who is seven and has just had his tonsils out.

'He is at the sweetest age,' he says. 'He was a bit frightened before being put to sleep. Two big tears rolled down, and when his mother bent down to kiss him he said: "Forgive me for the tears, mother. I didn't cry on purpose. Did it show?" "No," said his mother, "I was the only person to see them." "Then that's all right," he said. "I know you won't tell."

M

'We brought him back in the evening, and I said to him:

'"You will sleep with your mother, and I will sleep in the nursery with your little brother who might be afraid to be alone." When I went into the nursery he had arranged his teddy bear for me in his little bed; its head was on the pillow, and the arms nicely out on the sheet.

'My wife was a professor herself, and when I was at Colditz she took my place, but now she has given up her practice to look after us. I adore my wife, my family, and my calling. By the way, I have a hobby. Like so many busy men all over the world, I have taught myself to paint. I have a little cottage not too far out of Paris so that even during my holidays I can be at the hospital within an hour if I am needed urgently. Perhaps as a result of my captivity at Colditz, I feel a need to live intensely, and I love everything—Paris, the cinema, music, the theatre, good food!'

Here we are in front of the Plaza-Athénée—impressively uniformed porters, Cadillacs, swing doors, thick carpets.

Dr Hofmann sees our mutual friend, Georges Marin, through the half-open door of his office, and says to me:

'There is a man who is always busy. I hope he is as happy in his job as I am in mine. We were three years at Colditz, three years of enforced idleness. Isn't that a terrible indictment of our politicians! I think we all became a little mad at Colditz, but it's now our old school tie. We stick together. Last week the wife of a very important man came to me with an introduction from a famous specialist who was also at Colditz. There were two words on the card, "*grosses bises*" (big kisses), and my patient was appallingly shocked. I think she found it hard to believe that we were serious doctors!'

CHAPTER XIX

NOW HERE I am in the Louvre, very tired, and seated in front of the Joconde.

I feel a little guilty because, on account of the Joconde, my back is most unwillingly turned upon Leonardo da Vinci's other masterpiece, the portrait of the beautiful Francis I.

An attendant arrives and takes up his post on the right of my settee. A few moments later a second attendant arrives from the opposite direction and posts himself on my left.

I have a horrible feeling that I am quietly being placed under arrest. I would desperately like to tell them that I have no intention whatever of stealing the Joconde. Each of the attendants takes three paces to the rear. They are now behind me—between me and the chevalier king Francis I. Something unpleasant runs down my spine. I listen intently for any sound.

Then I hear:

'The beans were excellent in the canteen to-day— and incidentally, I saw thy daughter looking for thee. I hear she has passed her examination, and she was anxious to tell thee. Didst thou see her?'

'No, I did not see her, but now that thou tellest me that she has passed her examination, I am right glad.'

The last speaker takes three paces forward, looks suspiciously round, and quietly slips away.

'Are you watching me in case I steal the Joconde?' I ask the remaining attendant.

'No,' he answers, 'but we are not allowed to go into each other's hall and gossip. The settee you happen to be occupying makes a frontier post. I suppose, madame, that our few private remarks did not prevent you from enjoying your view of the Joconde?'

'Not at all.'

'I have only been an attendant here for a short time. Before that I was a soldier. We do a few months in each hall to get to know the pictures by name, but this hall is the most closely guarded—because of *her*.'

He winks at the Joconde.

'I found it hard at the beginning to get accustomed to the jargon. The head attendant, for instance, would say to me:

'"You are for the Joconde to-day."

'When I was here, people would come up and ask to be directed to the Mona Lisa, and I would scratch my poor head, and say to myself: "I've heard that name, but where?"

'I was worried, madame. I hate to look silly. I come from that part of France where the men are proud. A colleague said to me one day:

'"What's on your mind? Are you in trouble with some woman?"

'"Yes, in a way," I said. "Who is this Mona Lisa?"

'"In front of you," he answered. "The one with the curious eyes."

'"Don't pull my leg," I said. "That's the Joconde."

'"They are the same," he explained. "We didn't tell you. We thought you knew. This Mona Lisa was the wife of the Florentine Francesco del Giocondo. Da Vinci worked four years on that picture, without finishing it to his satisfaction."'

We both look intently at the Joconde.

'Well,' I ask at last, 'what do you think of her?'

'I think it must be true about her eyes,' he says thoughtfully; 'but on account of her I was made to feel small, and that's a thing for which I can't forgive a woman!'

CHAPTER XX

THIS IS delightful. I have just had lunch with an American: in a few moments a Frenchman is to take me to the races at Longchamp.

The American was the food buyer for a New York department store. Men work very hard, but if they are clever they organize their lives so that they have a much easier time than we do. This was a very tidy little man, both in thought and person. His life's battle is to find new and intriguing delicacies for the great American public, and his battleground is all that part of Europe which is not Russian and the more inhabited parts of North Africa. He told me that his most recent achievement was to arrange for wood strawberries to be picked in the morning at Orleans, packed, rushed to Orly, and put on the night plane so that they can be served at lunch next day at the Colony Club in New York. I learned that the best wood strawberries in France are grown round the city which Joan of Arc delivered from the English in the fifteenth century. I am rather excited to think that Orleans is adding to its fame, and it strikes me that the tiny French wood strawberry can blush deep red with pride to have become so internationally important.

What a lot of things this little man knew! Men pick up the most interesting information, and Americans are charming. I have always been happy in their company. This one intrigued me. He could eat the most delightful food, steaks and wood strawberries, but no, he ordered bacon and eggs, coffee and fresh cream in a large cup, and I reflected that we all of us reveal our nationalities more quickly by the food we eat than by our passports. However, my host was a gastronomic encyclopaedia. My eyes opened wide when he talked about caviare, truffles, and *foie gras*. He knew all the best wines of my country. His journeys lead him through romantic corners of France but for him there are no flights or digressions from work. He would not be tempted away into the mossy paths of fantasy. His love of wood strawberries is purely objective.

For this reason, I repeat, men have an easier time than we do. They work to schedule. At the end of a hard day they go to the theatre. The next morning they are back at work. A woman who seeks to live that kind of life, and in these days many do, must go to the hairdresser, think about what she will wear. All this, I own, is charming. But we have the dual fatigue of our profession and the normal business of being a woman.

My friend is taking an ocean liner back to New York so that he can have a rest, a real vacation, he said, before facing again the strain and competition of life in New York. So he will sleep, sleep for hours on the liner going over. On the other hand, when he comes to Europe, he flies, because he claims that a business man cannot get down to a new job too quickly: it is only when he has accomplished what he set out to do that he can take a long and lazy trip back.

Well, good luck to you, New York food buyer, and I hope you sleep and sleep. I have always dreamed of arriving at New York past the Statue of Liberty. Each time I have gone there it has been by way of Montreal and the Delaware and Hudson. I dream of the Statue of Liberty because it is the dream of all little girls in Europe. People tell me that ocean liners are now so large that they dwarf the statue, that newcomers no longer feel the thrill of the early emigrants. My grand-

father, and Bartholdi who make the statue, were both
born in Colmar; and my grandfather's sister emigrated to
America in 1872. For these reasons I desire once in
my life to look upon the statue from the deck of a liner,
and experience the poignancy of the nineteenth-century
emigrant.

Here I am with my Frenchman at Longchamp!

The racecourse is green, pretty, and home-like. I am
continually amazed by the countrified sights that Paris
has to offer, and by the fact that the city has reconciled
democracy and beauty. The trees are so large and
leafy that during a sudden shower we remain perfectly
dry under the shelter of one of them. The racing to-day
is for experts. I have never seen so many men. My
companion puts a lot of money on each race. I do not
follow his example. However, there is an English
horse with whose owner I once went cruising on the
Arandora Star. Did ever a ship made for laughter and
romance end more tragically? I put a little money on
the horse, but it comes in second. We go to the grand-
stand to watch the races; we return to the paddock to
watch the horses being led in. We took less than ten
minutes to reach this glorious sporting print set in the
verdant clearing of a thick wood. We take the car and
in another five minutes reach the Trianon Palace at
Versailles. Is there anything more beautiful in the
whole world? This is a corner of paradise and I would
like to wake up in the morning in the stillness of this
royal seat. We drive to Marie Antoinette's *hameau*
where she came to rest from her queenly duties. Here
we are truly in the depths of the country. Nothing is
in any way less beautiful now than in the days of the
kings and queens of France. A gingerbread vendor
who might have walked out of a child's picture-book a
century and a half ago folds up his little table, scatters

what remains of his stock-in-trade on the gravel path, and limps away. Two robins who have been watching him from a holly bush, and waiting eagerly for his departure, fly down and gorge on gingerbread and sugar icing. Then they hop on the seat where the vendor sat. A *gardien de la paix* comes along on a bicycle and asks if we have seen two young men about. We tell him that we have only seen a gingerbread vendor and two robins. A schoolmistress comes along with a bevy of little girls whose shrill cries echo for a moment through the woods, then die away.

We return to Paris and dine at the Cabaret. There are many Americans, extremely elegant, and the dinner makes one realize that Paris alone has not allowed its gastronomic tastes to deteriorate. We have enjoyed, I feel, the perfectly balanced day—half in country, half in town. Like New York, Paris builds skywards, but in her case to save her woodlands from being devoured.

CHAPTER XXI

'WOMEN,' says Annie, 'are curious, and least reasonable, when they buy a dress. They will pay vast sums for a model by Maggy Rouff or Jacques Fath, and the next moment ask me, in a whisper, for the address of a little dressmaker round the corner. I have in this little black note-book the names and addresses of little dressmakers who are geniuses. Believe me, Madame Henrey, I know about these things.'

I call her 'Annie Get Your Customer'—this young woman, dark and extremely pretty, who looks after the show-cases at the Plaza-Athénée. She is a female commander-in-chief with the luxury trades of Paris as her troops. Half a dozen telephone calls will bring to your apartment seamstresses, modistes, lingerie-makers, bag-makers, furriers, jewellers.

She is looking up at me from behind two beautiful eighteenth-century silver candlesticks, and I ask her what she is doing with them.

'But, madame,' she says plaintively, as if there could be any doubt about it, 'I hope to sell them. One is simply obliged to understand, that the days of big wealth are not likely to come back during our lives. There was once a maharajah who was in such a hurry to give a pretty girl a diamond bracelet he saw in an hotel show-case that he broke the glass and said to the manager: "Put this trinket on my bill."

'There are no maharajahs left. All the same, these show-cases represent what is most beautiful in Paris, and that is a tremendous thing to say, for the luxury of things feminine in Paris remains the most fabulous in the world. The famous houses who maintain cases here realize the peculiar value of our clients. They treat them with the utmost politeness, for they know that the woman who comes here this summer is almost certain to come back in a year's time. I have many women from the most distant parts of the globe who buy a bag, for instance, and then bring it back to be altered or re-covered, and you may be certain that the firm will make any sacrifice to oblige them.

'My best customers are often women who have been out all day with their husbands visiting Versailles or Chantilly, and are then too exhausted to go shopping before dinner. That is my opportunity. I can find them instantly a dress, a hat, a bag, gloves, a fur, the loveliest diamonds from the rue de la Paix.

'Has it always been my job? No, I am really a masseuse. I came here to take the place of a girl friend who was on holiday. Then she married and I took over.

'As you say, Spanish is important. They are immensely flattered, especially the Mexicans. They consider it a politeness to begin the conversation in their own tongue; afterwards one can slip into French or English.

'When I was a little girl I had a passion for railroad stations. I liked to see people coming and going. I still like it. I do not know what it is to keep set hours, for my best moments are during the lunch period and at night. Therefore, if it is necessary, I gladly stay till midnight. Why should I complain if I am here to make money? But, in fact, I love it. The customers are delightful and the hotel staff charming. People are so wrong to think of jobs as being necessarily dull. I feel like a hostess who might have an At Home every day of the week.

'Of course, I am not married. That makes a difference. But I have my parents to spoil, and that's great fun. For instance,' she cries suddenly, as she unpacks a box of men's ties from a famous hosier, 'this tie would suit my father admirably. I shall buy it for him at the end of the week. It's lovely to have a father to spoil, but though I am patient with women customers, I can't stand selling ties to men. It's amazing what a long time men take to make up their minds. They will unfold a hundred ties, and leave everything upside-down.

'One needs to be young and strong. Those show-cases by the English Bar, for instance. It is my job to keep them clean, and you should see me at the top of a ladder with a duster in my hand! I ruin all my dresses but I don't worry much about clothes. It would put the women against me. If I were to be too elegant, they wouldn't trust me any more, and when their husbands came to buy some trifle for them, it would make complications. Good temper is the best commodity for a girl in my line of business. To be always smiling. To laugh and chat with customers even if they don't buy anything. You may think that's obvious. Perhaps, but it took me three years to learn it, Madame Henrey.

'Life for a girl is such tremendous fun when she realizes it.

'The other day we had a new page-boy. A customer called him and said: "Sonny, call me a taxi and tell him to take me to the Cunard." The little French page-boy thought he wanted to see the *canards*—the ducks. It was pouring, and the taxi-driver took his fare all round the Bois de Boulogne, cruising slowly along the lake-side while the unfortunate man kept repeating: "La Cunard! La Cunard!" "Yes, monsieur," answered the taxi-driver. "Beautiful *canards*. We go round again, yes?"

'What is nice about the Americans is that they all try to talk French. Some of the young women speak it very well. Those who don't know a word the day they arrive are not afraid to plunge into it. They ask one for the Avenue Victor Vous Allez for the Avenue Victor Hugo, and a Bostonian had us all guessing when she wanted to be driven to Candle Valley, which turned out to be Bougival!

'No, work in a big hotel is fun. Romance of some kind or other is always just round the corner. It's in the big stores that the girls work hard because they are almost exclusively dealing with customers who never have enough money, and who accordingly think they can find a way to make the little they have buy twice as much as it should. They make you open everything— and nine times out of ten leave without making a purchase, whereas the rich woman is not only in a good temper but has been taught that she must be polite with a salesgirl.

'People say that rich women are bored. I don't believe it. There's a *chansonnier* in Montmartre just now who looks at his audience and asks: "Ah! Now tell me something! Rich people—they drive about in nice cars, they go to Deauville, they go to Monte Carlo, they go to Switzerland for the winter sports, but do you think they amuse themselves?"

'Long pause, and then the *chansonnier* adds triumphantly:

'"But of course they amuse themselves! They have a lovely time!"

'And of course the audience roars with laughter, because if we were rich we would probably do all the things they do. And then why should we be bad-tempered?

'When I was younger I wanted terribly to be married. Well, it just didn't work out that way, not yet at all events. Perhaps it's a good thing I didn't marry rashly, in a hurry. A girl changes. She quickly develops an interest in whatever she is doing. Adaptability is our strong point. I might not be happy now tucked away in some suburb. When I was still a masseuse a fortune-teller said to me: "Nothing you have done up till now has satisfied you. I see mirrors, lots of them, and gold leaf. That is where you will be happy."

'To sell successfully here I simply had to learn about the things I was trying to sell. That's what I like about my job. There are diamond pieces here worth many thousands. What a fool I would be not to learn all about these lovely stones, even though I may never own one myself. I could hardly tell mink from sable when I came here. That wanted learning too—and about dressmaking and about hats. Each is a profession in itself. To find out about them is as much fun for a girl as to learn about motor-cars is fun for a man. And this job is exciting, the fact that when I arrive in the morning I have no idea whether I shall sell a mink stole, a handkerchief, or maybe nothing all day. Some days I make several thousand francs. Some days I go home without the bus fare, but that's what I like. I'm kept alert, on my toes. So I remain young and gay.

'Then there are the people I meet, the people in the different trades who end by respecting me because I have learnt to sell intelligently the things they are so proud to have made. I know hundreds of people now, many of them with magical names. I can more or less talk to Dior. That's something for a girl in an hotel, isn't it? What young woman wants a steady job? When we are not rich we want to climb out of it. I see you like the little blouse in that show-case. It costs a fortune.'

'I'm not surprised. Look at the tiny pleats in the

collar. Tell me this, Annie Get Your Customer. Could a little dressmaker do this sort of work?'

She looks puzzled.

'I don't know,' she answers truthfully. 'I'm not certain she could manage anything as complicated as that. What are you driving at? You mean that I was wrong to pretend that the little dressmakers whose names I have in my note-book and who, I claimed, were geniuses, could do as well as the great fashion houses? I suppose you are right. The great houses inspire fashion: the cleverest little dressmaker merely follows. On the other hand, it's not always easy to make a customer appreciate unusual work. One needs to be an expert.'

'But you said you wanted to learn.'

'You're trying to catch me out!' she exclaims. 'But seriously, you know what customers are! They are so easily influenced by colour, and by the way a blouse stands up in a show-case. This one, for instance, really looks as if it was being worn. The breasts are alive.'

'I agree, but you might not have been able to make the blouse stand up so attractively if it hadn't been for the cunning design?'

She looks at me darkly through her long lashes and smiles. Now she opens her hand-bag and counts her money. There are five 50-franc coins that look like gold. But of course they are imitation like so many other things that our governments provide us with these days.

'I put them in a milk bottle,' says Annie. 'When the bottle is full I know that I shall have five thousand francs, and that will go towards my holidays. I used to collect 20-franc pieces which are also in imitation gold, but one of my boy cousins, going through a suit belonging to his late father, found a real napoleon which

he brought me to sell for him. I put it in a corner of
my bag, but one night when it was raining, and I needed
small change to pay a cab, I passed it off in my hurry with
a lot of these metal coins. I would be intrigued to
know what the taxi-driver did with it. Did he give it
unknowingly to a fare? But this story taught me to
be careful. I had to pay my cousin four thousand
francs.'

CHAPTER XXII

JEAN-JACQUES GUERLAIN rings up to know why I did not let him drive me home after Monick Boucheron's cocktail-party. He says he has to go to his factory this morning, and what am I doing? Writing letters? Why, I would do far better to leave the letters unanswered and come and see how perfume and face-powder are made! It's a beautiful morning and he will drown me in 'Heure Bleue.' That settles it. I leap out of bed.

This young man with the celebrated name is tall and very elegant. We drive to Courbevoie. The factory, he says, is absolutely new and built on land where there have not been any factories before. The old one was blown up in an allied bombing raid. Unfortunately it had stood near another factory engaged on war work for the Germans. The war factory was left standing and the cosmetics blown up.

The factory is white, and we are no sooner in the courtyard than the air seems perfumed. In the laboratory, wearing a white coat, is M. Guerlain *père*, a big dog lying at his feet. This patriarchal scene surprises. One has ceased to think of factories in terms of families but this is a family picture, the grave-looking father and his dog. The old gentleman welcomes me very courteously. His dog rises and licks my hand. Another son is here also, in white like his father. They are very pleased that I should have come with Jean-Jacques. They hope I will make myself at home, do just as I please. While speaking, the father mixes essences, shakes tubes, furrows his fine brow, searches for the next perfume that will break upon the world. Sometimes his dog flops down on the floor, but as soon as the master moves more than a few paces away, the dog rises and follows. Father and son have suddenly gone over to a large case of ambergris. They peer into it. So does the dog, wagging his tail. I would like to be a painter and commit this scene to canvas, modern alchemists working, not to manufacture gold, but to discover new artifices for feminine seductiveness. Ambergris, I seem to recall from schoolgirl days, is a wax-like secretion of the sperm whale. I ask rather timidly if my memory is correct. Jean-Jacques is more poetical. As we join the group and he plunges his fine young hand amongst the uneven-looking pebbles, he says: 'These things are found strewn over golden sand on distant beaches, the result of some stomach illness of the fantastic cachalot. We think he dies from his malady, but in dying he leaves us this wax-like pebble so necessary for the mixture of rare perfumes.'

The father, the two sons, the dog, and myself move quietly amongst essences some of which link us with the Italian and French Renaissance. I recall the little shoemaker of the rue Clément Marot. He, his narrow picturesque shop, and his street also set me dreaming of the Renaissance. Once more fragments of the poems of Clément Marot, Marguerite de Valois, and Ronsard jostle in my ears, and an old print of Erasmus, seen on the quays, causes me to picture M. Guerlain *père* in a robe and a pancake hat. Alchemists are always searching for an elixir. This fine old gentleman, aided by his two sons, is a reincarnation of the Middle Ages, searching painstakingly for the luxurious in a hard, atomic world.

Fat bottles in leather jackets contain bergamot from a curious Italian lemon, musk, benjoin, and jasmine of which this single bottle contains the equivalent of half a

N

million flowers. A round table has compartments in which stand precious phials with names that invoke in my mind the days of knight-errants. I find here some extract of violets which, I am astounded to learn, unlike jasmine, men have never been able to obtain in natural form from the flower whose perfume is apparently too delicate to be captured alive. So this is synthetic. Certain bottles are opened for me and I am invited to smell, but I soon realize that the alchemist is obliged to mix his treasures very cunningly before they flatter our senses.

On the wall is a portrait of grandfather Guerlain. He is riding a horse and looks down with pride at his son and his grandsons so busily at work. He died in his ninety-third year.

I terribly want to see how my face-powder is made, and Jean-Jacques leads me there. The great drums surprise me, and even more the urns in which pieces of rounded glass break up the exquisite pastel shades that will give the soft, pearly texture to our complexions. How slow and regular is the pounding of the glass which, untiringly as the sea, continues to beat upon the colour! Above each urn is the date when the machine was put into motion. One of them has been crushing delicate pink every day for six months. Here is an art in which men are not hurried. The combination of age-old secrets and unhurried work surprises and delights. One thinks of Nefertiti with her amber skin and painted eyes, of the pots of make-up buried in Egyptian tombs, of the perfumes brought across the sea in oared ships to Greek courtesans, of the unchanging importance of perfumes and powders in an ever-changing world. Civilizations disappear, languages are forgotten, dynasties crash, empires are made and thrown away, but these aids to feminine allurement, taxed by politicians, scoffed at by the narrow-minded, eternally remain.

The very foundations of modern perfumery are the work of years, even of centuries, of life, of sunshine, of storms at sea and tides which bring up the ambergris of the cachalot. By way of retaliation these wonders, in turn, serve to exorcize the years in woman, to ward off the ravages of age, and to aid, by long experience, the budding rose to reveal its full glory.

'Before the First World War,' says Jean-Jacques, 'there were only men in the factory. The door-keeper was the only woman. Now there are only a few men— my father and my brother in the laboratory, the men who look after the furnaces. All the rest are women.

'Here, for instance, is what we call the fairies' kitchen. Did you not tell me in the car just now that you always use the face cream "Secret de Bonne Femme"? Here it is being stirred in a magic cauldron by two good fairies, dispensers of eternal youth.'

Yes, indeed, here is the cream as pure as snow! How good it smells! How expertly stirred! How curiously whipped with a blade into the little glass jars, as dark as night, which I have known and loved since I was a little girl.

The crystal bottles destined for the perfumes are being washed in rain-water collected from the roof. The packing-room is a dream. Packing-cases are ready to leave for every part of the globe. I read: Rome, Wiesbaden, Hong Kong, Habana, Bayreuth, Mexico City; and each bears the words MADE IN FRANCE in large black letters. If ever I meet one of these cases in my wanderings round the world I shall think of M. Guerlain *père*, his dog, his two elegant sons, and all those shining crystal bottles of 'Heure Bleue,' 'Mitsouko,' 'Fleur de Feu,' 'Atuana,' 'Sous le Vent,' patiently waiting to be packed in quilted boxes, done up in blue paper, stamped with the colours of France, and sent off to lovely women in distant lands who will allow the magic perfume lightly to scent their blonde or dark hair, to kiss the backs of their ears, to settle like dew on a newly ironed blouse, so that as they move about they will leave behind them the subtle trail of French genius and civilization.

Midday rings. Young packers in sky-blue pinafores jump up from long tables. Jean-Jacques and I are surrounded by laughing, joking, light-footed girls and women. An appetizing odour of steak and fried potatoes rushes towards us from the canteen whither all these people are bound, and is met by a barrage of 'Mitsouko' and 'Heure Bleue'! Oh, happy, feminine world.

On my return to the Plaza I find the Frenchman who had taken me to the races at Longchamp waiting for me in the hall. He is now anxious to show me the Utrillos at Pétridès. These, he explains, are the Utrillos of the good period, churches of very pure white with the rue Saint-Vincent and the long cemetery wall. Inspired by these pictures, I tell him of my expedition to the rue de Sévigné and of my disappointment at finding the Carnavalet Museum closed. 'Let's go!' he immediately exclaims.

He has parked the car just off the Boulevard Haussmann, but not being very certain how to get to the rue de Sévigné, and mistrusting my sense of direction, he decides to make inquiries. Taxi-drivers, he says, are the people to ask. They are very good at explaining the quickest route across Paris. The one he picks has never heard of the Carnavalet, swears that the rue de Sévigné does not exist, and that the Place des Vosges must have been recently named. I repeat with some satisfaction that he has merely to drive and that I will guide him. I am by now very well acquainted with the streets round the Bazar de l'Hôtel de Ville, and my mirror is now a trusted friend on my dressing-table.

I find it ironical that the municipality of Paris should

have turned Mme de Sévigné's former house into a
museum of revolutionary relics. One is shown the
last shirt worn by the unfortunate Louis XVI before
being led to the guillotine, the mandrel lathe on which
he made his keys, and a collection of Marat's razors!
Upon these objects Mme de Sévigné and her daughter
Mme de Grignan, to whom she wrote her famous
letters, look with calm indifference, as if relieved to
think they both died nearly a century before these
horrors happened.

The gardens at the back of the house with the box-
tree geometrical designs are quite beautiful, whilst the
street in front is so utterly medieval that one reflects
that the whole of Paris is a living, throbbing museum.
From the Place de la Bastille comes the lilting music of a
fun fair, giving one the itch to dance.

'Well,' says my companion, 'these are things I
should never have done with a real Parisienne, and yet
I have enjoyed every moment. One day, as a return
compliment, I will take you to Sèvres, for porcelain has
become my passion. Until a short time ago I knew
absolutely nothing about it, but now these tiny figurines
worth hundreds of pounds that you can hold in the palm
of a hand bewilder and fascinate me.

'The other morning on my return home after a night
of revelry—in Paris we start rather late in the evening
but seldom return before daylight—I looked everywhere for my tooth-paste. I wandered from room to
room in the flat, opening drawers I had never opened
before. My wife was away, and I talked inanely to
myself: "Where on earth have I put this tooth-paste?
Surely nobody has walked off with it?" I was angry.
I felt abandoned. One likes to air one's grievances to a
wife. Yet a few hours earlier I had felt very manly and
self-reliant, for I was with a lot of other men, business
associates, drinking brandy in a night-club. Ah, what

was this? No, not my tooth-paste, but a very similar
tube on which was written "Shampoo." It must have
belonged to my wife. I squeezed some out and it
smelt good. I put some on the toothbrush and brushed
my teeth. "This stuff is marvellous!" I thought—
and at this moment I happened to look at my most
recent acquisition, a porcelain shepherdess. I was not
very sure of myself when I bought her, but a collector,
at the beginning, is bound to take risks, to back his
judgment. Only it's a costly business with old china
when your judgment proves faulty, because you can
drop a lot of money. I thought she might look better
for a shampoo. The stuff had been quite amazing on
my teeth. I shampooed the little lady all over. The
result was astounding. I took her to another dealer
who offered me twice what I had paid for her. I am
now using the shampoo for cleaning old masters.
They become quite luminous. I don't know what the
Louvre would say, but it's my opinion that the charm
of modern painting is its luminosity. What do you
think?

'Well now,' he continues, looking at his watch, 'I
have two cocktail-parties and a dinner engagement.
I must drive you home.'

I will not stay at home doing nothing. I will telephone Véra Korène who is my neighbour on the roof-
tops.

'Oh!' she cries. 'I'm just back from a matinée.
You know what Thursdays are like at the Comédie
Française, mostly children and students, a terribly
earnest, serious audience with the theatre full from top
to bottom. I am done in, and as hungry as a tigress.
Shall we have dinner together in the buttery?'

She arrives, draped in a large red coat with wide
sleeves, and one would need to be as consummate an

artist as she is to pass through a packed room, head held high, without brushing against a table.

'*Ouf*, my dear! I'm dead! These matinées take it out of me. I am terrified when I have to play before young people. In tragedy especially. A tragic gesture pushed a fraction too far can start ironic laughter. Children are tremendously shrewd and quite without pity. Their most dangerous moment—for us—is when they are emerging from childhood into adolescence. I can feel my pulse beating furiously as soon as I have to go on and face them. They frighten me also because I like them, and realize how their first impressions, especially if they are boys, are likely to remain with them throughout life.

'I once consulted a famous doctor on what I should do to overcome stage fright. He gave me this naïve advice:

'"Madame," he said, "try to imagine, when you make your entry, that the theatre is full of children!"

'I do not doubt that this doctor is brilliant as a medical man, but you see that he gave me, with the most complete assurance, advice that proved him to be as ignorant about the theatre as I am about medicine. This experience taught me that one should never ask anybody for advice.

'You would not believe,' she goes on, 'how unfathomably timid I, a career woman, am in the presence of boys. Girls are different. I remember what I was like, and after all, girls are ourselves in embryo, but a boy is incredibly different. As soon as I come anywhere near them, I make myself as insignificant as possible. Then I ask them to do something for me, to render me a service.

'When I was in America I was very shy with adolescent young men. They appeared to know so many things. I would ask them to fill up forms and to help me with various formalities which, quite honestly, I was incapable of understanding. This turned them into staunch friends and, in point of fact, I was doing them a kindness by judging them capable of helping me.

'I think it essential that boys should be taught very young how to treat women. I realize how tiresome it must be for a little boy, full of energy, to efface himself before a woman, but the movement should be instinctive, learned from boyhood.

'I have a small nephew to whom I explained that I was very frightened of a man sitting at a large desk. I wondered if he would be brave enough to go up and ask this man for a detail I needed about a stage costume. My nephew was very proud to do this for me. When a boy feels he is protecting somebody, he will do almost anything.

'From time to time I fetch him at college. "Do you see that little girl?" he said to me one Thursday. "She is an orphan, and has no right to go out."

'"Not even if we invited her?"

'"No," he answered importantly. "I made inquiries."

'My nephew and I had a charming lunch, after which:

'"Shall we find something for the little girl who cannot go out?" I asked, and I took a box and put some *marrons glacés* and *petits fours* into it; "and look!" I exclaimed. "Look at this pretty ribbon with which she will be able to tie up her hair when she goes to sleep at night. There is nothing so pretty as a little girl asleep with a ribbon in her hair. The ribbon looks like the petals of a rose."

'I noticed a gleam in his eyes. He was visualizing the little girl and the rose petals.

'"You know," I went on, "because little girls are not so strong as little boys, they busy themselves with ribbons and with other things that appear stupid to strong, healthy boys like you.   But that is life."

'He was immensely interested.

'In the theatre I am the embodiment of energy and self-confidence, but in everyday life I am placid and shy.   I cannot drive a motor-car.   Anything vaguely mechanical terrifies me.   But as soon as I am on the stage I lose every trace of timidity.   I am audacious. In *Coriolanus* I lead a crowd of five hundred who look to me for every movement.   I make them do exactly what I want.

'At one time the bitterest of the stage fighting was cut out, notably a duel with short, heavy swords which some people thought was too revoltingly cruel, but which I, a feeble woman, think admirable.   I love to see a battle, to watch men fighting.   Feminine women admire soldiers, and though I agree that this is certainly not a sign of intelligence, it is quite definitely a sign of femininity.   The actors who are to revive this rather terrible duel have been practising for a month and a half.   We are drawing up the details of this fight as meticulously as Diaghilev drew up the details of a new ballet or the electricians paint the sky with the right glow for a burning house or a blood-stained battle-field.

'A love scene, for instance, requires not merely thought but intuition.

'I have reached a sufficient eminence in my profession to say to a partner in rehearsal:

'"Allow me, but I much prefer your hand here . . . than there."'

Mme Korène acts this scene over the dinner table, with movements gentle and possessive.

'Do I not know,' she continues, 'what movement, what caress, gives me most pleasure in real life?   How can a stage director, who is a man, presume to know how I, a woman, and one particular woman at that, react to the touch of a lover's hand? Men have much to learn from women in the art of love.

'On the other hand I acknowledge their undoubted good taste.

'My most beautiful dresses, those in which I have earned applause, have been chosen by men. Men choose admirably for women, and when a woman has a husband who is not interested in what she wears, the chances are that she will be badly dressed.

'I don't think carnations bring one bad luck. On the other hand, people in the theatre consider green an unlucky colour. If an actress is asked to wear a green dress, or if a set has preponderance of green, the troupe is apt to murmur. I am happiest in white. As soon as I am in a white dress, I open out. That is the exact word, I open out. I break into a new world. White liberates me. Actors are always nervous, and most of them, contrary to popular belief, are very religious. I was called upon one evening, during a gala performance of the ballet, to sit in the presidential box, which is almost on the stage. I could see the ballet-dancers pause for a moment in the wings and make the sign of the cross before coming on. I also make a quick prayer before every entry.

'The Comédie Française is a peculiar institution. In other countries a good actress will appear in a play, and then wait some time for another. She may even go off for a long period to New York or Hollywood. But the Comédie Française is a permanent affair. The actress becomes an established personage and what is done in the theatre assumes an official importance.

'In the revival of *Coriolanus* I shall omit the Roman salute which has recently left too many poignant and cruel memories in the hearts of our people; but it is only safe to omit something if you are perfectly aware of its existence. The law is an example of what I mean. If a lawyer is thoroughly conversant with legal procedure, he can often get round a law, but he must know precisely what he is doing.

'As often as possible I consult a very distinguished classical scholar who is my friend. I ask him to explain with great patience various aspects of that Roman life which he, poor man, only knows from books. I wanted to discover, for instance, for one of my scenes, if the Roman people could be present at debates in the Senate. "Of course," he answered, "but the Senate took care to discuss what was really important in secret beforehand."

'What helps me greatly at the Comédie Française is an ear for music.

'One must put rhythm into one's silences. One must learn to cry, like the Virgin Mary in paintings by the great Italian masters, without leaving a trace of tears. Tears should fall from the eyes like pearls. I received my Societyship to the famous troupe on the strength of a *silent* part.'

'Though you are still so young,' I ask, 'have you been married?'

'Yes, I was married. It is almost part of my profession, alas, to be married and separated. I would willingly enough have renounced the theatre for married life—we women never feel we have enough to give—but it did not work out that way.

'I am vitally interested in the people I meet. I know beforehand that they will have great failings, as indeed I have, but as I am not obliged to live with them, I am only interested in their qualities.

'I have a strong will. When we go on tour I fight

against illness. I have just come back from Tunisia. The distances are tremendous, the variations of temperature considerable, and the food difficult to digest. One can never take a risk in my profession.

'I used to liken myself to a galloping mare—for I was obliged to cover long distances in such heat that I was in a continual sweat, and when I arrived at my destination I had to have a rug thrown over my shoulders, as if I were a horse!

'But when, in the evening, I saw audiences made up of people who had come hundreds of miles to see the classics played in French, I forgot the discomforts. On our return to Orly aerodrome I found myself saying thank you to customs officers and aerodrome officials who all went out of their way to make things easy for me, for they knew that in a few hours I would be playing in de Montherlant's *Pasiphaé*, for which part I need more than an hour to dress my hair, and that for a woman who has been flying through the clouds from North Africa to Paris, the earth when she sets foot on it again is full of pitfalls!

'Acting frees my soul.

'I can shout, hurl insults, witness the foulest murders, and commit adultery. It is a way of ridding myself of base instincts.

'Conversely my femininity robs me of any desire to be independent.

'I like the man to choose the wine, to plan my evening. Let him do whatever pleases him. I will obey. My mother, whom I adore, taught my sister and me to be loving servants of my brother and if, as she sometimes did, she asked us to brush his suit or clean his shoes, we thought that quite normal. She was right. The menial tasks lift a woman's natural charm to great heights. If you ask the little boy to carry the little girl's parcel because it is heavy, then it is right for the girl to sew on his buttons. Women who try to copy men are seldom loved. They become good companions and that, for a woman, is to be treated with indifference.'

What a lovely ending to my day!

Véra Korène's voice, grave and modulated, is music. She turns to me suddenly and asks:

'Why don't you write me a play?'

At times this amazing actress reminds me of my darling Paloma who, capricious genius, confined her play-acting to the Green Park and the London streets round the British Museum.

To write a play for Véra Korène?

'Ah! If only I could!'

CHAPTER XXIII

JEANNE and I jump lightly on a Montmartre bus in front of Christian Dior's. We are rather gay, having just lunched with a young woman from Brazil who has looked at us throughout the meal with eyes unbelievably beautiful and black. She had been married at sixteen and was only twenty-two, but what amazed Jeanne and me was her immense seriousness.

Naturally she adored Paris, but her enthusiasm was extremely poised. She had studied the city from two angles, the shops, which were her passion, and the restaurants and night-clubs where she had danced the samba. Her hands and wrists, which were of the smallest, jingled with pieces of eight whose red gold burned against her dark skin and, being narrow of hips and even narrower of waist, she was able to wear to advantage a thick tweed beige dress bought at Jacques Fath's *boutique*. Her eyes were so far apart that Jeanne and I, dynamic Frenchwomen, had the impression of looking into two large sleepy lakes, but we had no doubt that men would consider this sleepiness extremely seductive. Her dark appearance had so impressed itself upon me that when I looked at my own features in the mirror of my flapjack, I was shocked to see myself so blonde and pale.

We had grave fears during lunch that conversation might dry up altogether. Would Jeanne and I succeed in thinking up any new questions? We had come to the end of our favourite topics. Fashions had been fully explored. We had discussed every *boutique* in Paris. What made things worse was that our beautiful companion was neither hungry nor thirsty, for she lived by night and had not returned to the Plaza-Athénée till well after dawn.

She was to start off later in the day with friends on a motor tour in Spain, but she did not speak Spanish. The country, she thought, would be picturesque, but how could one tell in advance? Our lunch continued to drag. Jeanne, who is normally Etna in eruption, had told all her curious and amusing stories: the magnificent little creature between us continued peacefully to dream.

'What have you liked best in France?' we asked.

'Life,' she answered. *'La Vie.'*

'Life!' we echoed.

'Why yes,' she answered solemnly. 'Life. Life is gay but, more important still, it is never the same twice. That is what is so marvellous about Paris. I have decided that when I get back to Rio de Janeiro I shall have a long rest before returning to Paris next spring, for now that I know there is a season in Paris, I shall have to come back. Otherwise I would be thinking too much about it. Paris has only disappointed me in one thing, the shoe shops. Shoes are too expensive. In Rio we buy a lot of shoes, and they are very cheap.'

'Ah!' exclaimed Jeanne, warming up. 'Then I would love Rio, for I have a passion for shoes. There is a shop not far from here that specializes in small sizes, shoes for little feet, and they are cheaper than elsewhere. I heard this morning they were having a sale, and I hurried there full of joyful expectation. Imagine my disappointment when I discovered they were merely selling off the large shoes. There was nothing for me.'

Our Brazilian friend was slightly amused but she

added that it was surprising how easily women in Paris laughed. In Rio a woman did not laugh without a good reason. In Paris women laughed for no reason at all. That struck her as very curious. This truth having flown from her well-shaped lips, she proceeded to inform us that she had bought a great number of suitcases in which to pack all the things she had acquired in France, and that a woman friend was taking them to Rio in advance for her.

'We wear a great deal of black at home,' she said. 'Black is cool in hot weather. Do not peasant women in Latin countries dress in black? Oh, and I am very happy about the way they have done my hair in Paris. My hairdresser powders my hair over with blue. I find that extremely pretty.

'We have wonderful materials in Rio but oh! to find a dressmaker! That is the difficulty. We are reaching a point where textiles are becoming prettier and cheaper year by year, but fewer women know how to make a dress!'

We questioned her about servants in Brazil, and she said:

'Our mothers teach us when we are little girls to do a great many things ourselves, not because there is a shortage of servants but because one has to show them how to do everything. In South American countries, because of the heat, everything that is washable is continually being washed, so that one has to be careful what one leaves lying about. Women spend a great part of their lives washing, and gossiping while they wash, and the more they have to wash, the more they can gossip, but it is not good, as you can well imagine, to wash a dress from Balmain or Givenchy, so that is why I tell you that one has to be very careful what one leaves lying about!

'In Rio we dance a lot, and our lives mostly revolve

round a single commodity—coffee! Buyers come from all over the world, and we entertain them in our homes and country estates. Rio is growing enormously, and we have gone through many of the troubles of an expanding country, but now we notice with surprise that the once stable European countries have far more revolutions and political crises than we have. I have become much slimmer since I have been in Paris. There is so much to do, whereas in Rio I have very little to do except to take care not to put on weight.

'I am amazed how young women of forty look in Paris. And they are more than pretty—they look so healthy!'

We said farewell to our lovely South American flower in the hall of the Plaza, and as we hurried out into the Avenue Montaigne to catch our bus for Montmartre we felt liberated, as if we could now laugh as much as we liked without needing to furnish a reason for our happiness. We are bound for the market of Saint-Peter —*le marché de Saint-Pierre*—which is at the foot of the Sacré-Cœur.

My friend Jeanne spends several months every year at Nice where she was born and where she has a lovely house. When she is away from Nice one has the impression that something of her is missing. She is taking me to this market to buy cool cotton and linen dress materials for the summer holidays.

I reflect that it could hardly be hotter anywhere than it is in Paris to-day. People mill round us, and there are rolls and rolls of shantung, silk, linen, cotton, nylon, and terylene. A mist forms in front of my eyes. My head begins slowly to swim. When Jeanne suddenly asks me what I think of a material she is holding in her hand, I am incapable of giving her an intelligent answer. She buys the material, and overcome by a frenzy of

o

spending, declares her intention of going to the Galeries Lafayette to inspect the cotton dresses.

I feel better for this rapid return into Paris and we are surprised to find that there are not many people looking at seaside frocks. I adore being on the balcony of this magnificent shop, watching what is going on everywhere, upstairs as well as on the ground floor, even seeing the people crowded and motionless in the glass cages of the lifts that go up and down untiringly like yo-yos. I have got over the giddiness I felt in the heat of Montmartre. I am fascinated by all these people rushing about in the immense gilded store, but it is a friendly, happy crowd, not a frightening one.

We go to a café and sit down on the terrace. A crowd of men arrives, and they embrace one another with lusty kisses resounding from cheek to cheek.

'These,' declares Jeanne, 'are ex-prisoners from the same German camp. They derive fresh pleasures from each new meeting. My goodness! What a lot of embracing amongst men I have seen since the war! Four years in a German prison camp bound them together for ever with ties of friendship. My husband was telling me at breakfast about a young man he had sent to Germany to work. It was considered important for some reason that the young man should have this experience. The owner of the German firm, however, had been a prisoner of war in France and had been so badly treated that he hated the French. When my husband discovered this, he wrote to say that it might interest him to know that he, my husband, had spent several years in a German prison where he was constantly beaten and chained to other prisoners, and he added:

'"You can hardly ask me to pity you for whatever ill treatment you may have received from the French. You and I are merely victims of the war. Try not to be more bitter about it than I am."

'The German answered immediately.

'"Send your young Frenchman. I promise to treat him well."'

Jeanne adds:

'We who have known two wars are not quite like the others, even though the first war took place when we were little girls. For instance, when I was a very tiny girl I remember seeing the men who were blinded and gassed in the trenches of the First World War being driven in ambulances down the lovely Promenade des Anglais at Nice, and they were yelling with pain. Then also, during this war, our sunny Riviera went hungry to the point of starvation. It is a terrible thing when one lives in a part of the world which produces sunshine, blue sky, mimosa, carnations, but practically nothing to eat but olives, tangerines, and tomatoes, with the milk from a few lean cows. And here we are, you and I, talking about ways to keep slim. The bread for which we queued up and which then seemed, even in small quantities, like a gift from God, is now abundant and nicer than anywhere else in the world, and has become the enemy of the elegant woman. Are we not mad to discuss stupid things so seriously? We are too happy. That is the trouble.'

We take a bus as far as the Place de la Concorde, but it is a new type of bus in which the conductor sits at a desk in the centre: he presses a button and the doors open or close. By the introduction of these new buses one more source of charm disappears from the Paris streets. One can no longer unclip the leather lanyard at the back, clamber up the steps (helped by willing males), ride on the swinging observation platform, breathing the air of the streets, feeling the rain or the sun against one's hair, listening to the men talking as they smoke their Maryland cigarettes. Romance has gone. Automatic doors remain closed in traffic blocks, in front of red traffic lights. The conductor inside has become a human lever pushing automatic levers. The men cannot smoke. We are all obliged to sit down.

There is a great crowd in the Place de la Concorde. Many are waiting for an important person to emerge from the Hôtel Crillon. The red carpet is out, the Republican Guard are here in their lovely uniforms with the shining breastplates and the helmets with horse-hair. I say good-bye to Jeanne and decide to wait. Next to me is a very fat woman with a sleeping boy child in her arms: her little girl, unmindful of what the mother has come to see, plays happily on the edge of the red carpet but a *sergent de ville* with an eye on the regulations, leaves the ranks of drawn-up colleagues, lifts the little girl in his arms, and puts her back into the crowd. The red carpet is now clear. The important person will have it all to himself.

By and by the *sergent de ville* looks round. Where is the little girl he put back into the crowd? His eyes search for her. Ah, there she is, clutching her mother's skirt, her poor little face bathed in tears. The *sergent* breaks the ranks again, takes up the little girl a second time, and sits her down on the edge of the red carpet from which he had taken her up a few moments earlier, but this time he bends down and whispers something in her ear. The little girl smiles, and after that does not move.

'Present arms!'

Here comes the crown prince of Japan holding his silk hat upon which the sun makes play. I confess I find him enchanting. He is extremely smart. I recall the first lines of the Japanese national anthem:

> May our emperor's reign last one thousand years
>   And then another eight thousand,
> Until stones are turned into rocks
>   And moss grows thick.

The crown prince walks down the red carpet, suddenly

looks down at the little girl, smiles tenderly, and enters his car.

The show is over: the crowd disperses. The fat woman turns round and calls her daughter. She looks tired and the boy child in her arms is still asleep. Though the heir apparent of the Celestial Emperor allowed his shadow to fall momentarily across the infant's pale cheeks, the little boy will have no memories of this moment. He was fast asleep.

The Place de la Concorde is full of these tiny vehicles that make the buses appear monstrously large. The former Place Louis XV is a chaos of people and traffic. A young couple in love, looking so deeply into each other's eyes that they walk as if in a dream, suck alternately the same ice-cream, thus continuing the kiss still heavy on their lips. The statue of Albert I, King of the Belgians during the First World War, shines. The grass and the trees are splendidly green. The tricolour flies proudly from the Chamber of Deputies. There is no Government, but who cares?

Annie and her chief, seated together at Annie's little table, are gossiping. Annie's chief is as young as she is but is responsible for the combined show-cases of the Plaza-Athénée and the George V. As I am also seated in the hall I observe them, and listen from time to time to what they say. This is the most delightful spot in the hotel, for it allows one to inspect the smartest women in Paris as they come in and out, and having seen the collections of all the famous dressmakers, I can easily recognize the models they happen to be wearing.

Annie and her friend are extraordinary. Whereas I am an amateur, they are specialists. Their conversation reaches me in ascending and descending waves.

'That little dress from Jacques Fath's *boutique* is really a darling!'

'This one is *croquignolet*!'

'*Croquignolet*' is the name of a delightful pastry, a rather old-fashioned word which charms me when applied to a dress.

'Ah! That one is sensational, and worn by a really thunderous girl!'

This expression '*fille de tonnerre*' is the very latest ejaculation to describe the IT girl. Daughter of thunder —thunderous girl—to be beautiful, to be elegant, to call down upon one thunder and lightning!

Nowhere but in Paris does the feminine achieve such enthusiastic interest. One feels immense satisfaction in belonging to the sex that, on occasion, can split the heavens wide open. I cannot stand being alone any longer. I must go and join these two young women. They see me and exclaim:

'Sit you here beside us, Madame Henrey.'

The conversation veers in the direction of food, for Annie has discovered a restaurant where they know more than twenty different ways to cook frogs' legs. Chicken bathed in wine is another speciality of this house.

'I won't hear of these gargantuan meals,' says her chief. 'I have started to slim, and the mere sight of the menu of the George V is enough to make me falter in my resolutions. But have you noticed that whereas all the women in Paris are slimming, one encounters everywhere the most delicious odours of grilled rump steak and fried potatoes? Tell me also: are there any fewer cakes in the pastry-cooks'? Are you told that people no longer want butter or cream?'

Annie, whose chair is placed at exactly the right angle for her to see everybody coming through the swing doors of the hotel, cries out: 'My little ladies, prepare to witness a fine piece of "coachwork"!'

The piece of 'coachwork' is a famous mannequin.

I had already seen her when I was lunching at the
Relais with Jeanne, and I must immediately confess that
my admiration was cool. I thought her line superb.
She was slim without being bony, but I did not approve
of her legs or the way she walked, as if she were showing
off a dress in a fashion house. As she advances towards
us, our three pairs of eyes devour her. I find her no
more to my taste than at lunch-time. I think she
walks stupidly.

'If I were a man,' I hazard, 'I wouldn't like her legs.'

'I would be delighted to agree with you,' says Annie's
chief, 'but the men all think she is a daughter of thunder,
and the proof is that you never see her without a male
escort. You simply can't explain that away. She is
thunderous!'

'I admit that she is cover girl of *Vogue* or *Harper's*.
The hat is well balanced, the umbrella held like a
marshal's baton. She is very sure of herself.'

'Then again,' says Annie, 'she is always just right
whether you see her in the morning or in the afternoon.
At night she is *formidable*!'

Annie and her young chief are full of admiration. I
remain unrepentant. At this moment Cuny, the hall
commissionaire, who sees everybody, hears everything,
faithful sentinel, comes up to us and exclaims:

'What a woman! One doesn't see the likes of her
every day!'

Annie looks at me and says:

'Didn't I tell you that the men all think she's thunderous! I'm on your side secretly, but I wouldn't dare
say so.'

As soon as this whirlwind of elegance has passed on
her way, Annie resumes her discussions on gastronomy.
Rich women staying in the hotel often ask Annie to go
shopping for them. She hurries from dressmaker to
milliner, from shoemaker to blousemaker, and because

she is gay and quick expends so much energy in the
process, that she allows herself to be tempted by the
cakes in the pastry-cook's window.

'I buy a bun with chocolate spread,' she says, with a
look of greed in her eye, 'and I nibble it as I hurry along
the boulevard. My theory is that the walk counter-
balances the chocolate spread. I am like a schoolgirl
with my bun in my hand, tripping along, laughing at the
sunshine and the wind.'

'You're lucky to come to terms with your regime so
easily,' says her pretty chief. 'Rules are rules and I
keep them. Now, I am going to walk back to the
George V. You must come and see me there, Madame
Henrey. I do think it's lovely to work among beautiful things.'

Annie gets up to accompany her to what she calls the
'castle gates,' by which she means the baggage entrance
of the hotel. I suspect they have a few last-minute
secrets. Annie returns with a heart of lipstick im-
printed on her right cheek where her chief has kissed
her good-bye.

'It's so lovely working with young women of one's
own age!' she exclaims happily. 'Oh, life is such fun!'

A very corpulent man arrives.

He tells Annie he has been ill and has lost weight.
We are introduced. He is a journalist and has come to
interview Véra Korène, who is leaving this evening for
the festival at Lyons. The journalist has just come
back from an assignment in London, where he says that
the newspapers are all housed in immense palaces so
close to each other that they make a city of fairy palaces
and ink.

'In Paris,' he says, 'our newspaper offices often have
a provincial appearance. One goes up dark stairs in
buildings which seem to date from the Second Empire,

but there is romance about them, and the people who write in them retain a great deal of character, and are wonderful at talking and arguing.'

He disappears into the lift and Annie says:

'He's fat, isn't he?'

'Very fat.'

'I saw him the day he came back from Buchenwald. He was so thin you could see through him. He just escaped being fed into the furnace.'

We remain silent a moment. These sort of memories take the wind out of one.

'I am going to see Alex Maguy, the *couturier*,' I say to Annie. 'He is a man I have always wanted to know.'

'You are right to want to know him,' says Annie. 'He is the *couturier* who dresses the smartest women in Paris but whose name remains in the background. He is the Cardinal Richelieu of dressmaking. He is too big to want people to talk about him. Sobriety is his line. He lives in the rue Jean Goujon. Do you know where it is?'

'Yes,' I answer. 'I shall walk there. It is just behind the hotel in what I call my Renaissance quarter—Montaigne, Clément Marot, Jean Goujon—Goujon, the celebrated sixteenth-century sculptor who helped to decorate the Louvre.'

'There,' says Annie approvingly, 'you have taught me something.'

A beautiful house in this historic street, a house dignified with age, and a narrow stone staircase leading to plain doors—no light, no shop, not even one of those bronze or silver name-plates that expensive *couturiers* like to put outside their establishments.

There is a *salon* with chairs arranged for a show, but on the wall are amazing masterpieces by Braque, by Dufy, by Kisling, that are so luminous that they hurl colour in all directions, as if they had a surfeit of youth and daring. I am quite lost in admiration at the sight of these wonderful paintings hanging as if in a private house, not full of their importance, like old masters, but like a group of young men sitting round to smoke and talk. Though these great artists are no longer with us, haunting the streets of Montmartre, yet they are so recently gone that they and their works seem to us like contemporary good companions.

A salesgirl takes me up to Alex Maguy. I tell him that though we have not met before, I seem to have known him always, in the sense that so many Parisian women know him, because he has quietly influenced their lives.

'Yes,' he agrees. 'I have just presented my one hundred and fourth collection. If you divide by four, which is the number of collections I give each year, you will see that I have had this business in my blood for more than a quarter of a century. I only stopped working during the war. I was in Norway, and in a good many other places where there was fighting.'

I try to compute his age but he seems so much younger than the evidence of his record. He tells me that he is of Austrian origin and I look at the Gruau behind the desk at which he is seated—a crayon of a woman with reddish hair. He notices my interest, and explains:

'I am a tremendous enthusiast: that is why I am not popular with all the great men who suddenly decide to take up painting as a hobby. Painting is not a thing a man can do to rest a tired brain. These men would surely laugh at a painter who, to amuse himself, practised medicine or politics. There are, I read, seventy thousand people who paint and who live, more or less precariously, from the proceeds. Consider that out of these not twenty are known internationally. Everybody thinks he can do as well as Pablo Picasso. Alas, madame, genius is a rare thing.'

'Why are you so retiring, Monsieur Maguy?'

'I am always nervous. Each collection gives me intense stage fright. Then, quite honestly, I am not attracted by the limelight. I find other satisfactions more intense. That is why I live on the Quai des Orfèvres, at the very top of a house. My apartment has a wide balcony overlooking the Seine at its most historic and picturesque. I see the water, the trees, Notre Dame, and the Hôtel Dieu. I do not suppose there could be anything in the world more romantic than living on the top of a tower in the heart of medieval France. The moon lights up the towers of Notre Dame, and I can picture it as Victor Hugo painted it. I am so deeply moved every time I put the key into my apartment door, my heart beats so violently with pleasure, that I might be going to see a passionately loved mistress. My balcony almost touches the sky. I lean over it at night and dream.

'I love colours. I hate black. I very seldom include a black model in a collection: on the other hand, I confess that in summer when the sun plays on a woman's hair, especially if she is blonde like you, and on her skin, a black dress can be effective. South American women are right to wear black when the weather is hot, but almost anybody can make an effective black dress. It does not call for any particular genius.

'I dislike a lot of white round me. Thus I have a horror of sleeping between white sheets: they paralyse me, freeze me, give me the impression of being draped out for my funeral. Blue sheets are a corner of blue sky. I love them. They liberate my ideas. My thoughts fly about like happy butterflies.

'I admired Paul Poiret and Jean Patou enormously. These two names, especially the first, will grow in stature and will take an important place when the history of fashions comes to be written. They were both dazzling successes because they were both men in the real sense of the word and deeply in love with womankind. They dressed women superbly because, vulgarly speaking, they adored to undress them.'

'Monsieur Maguy,' I say, 'I suspect there are very famous dressmakers, both men and women, who cannot themselves sew or cut a dress. I have always been puzzled by this point. People say: "This man or that woman is a celebrated *couturier*," and add under their breath: "But they have never held a needle in their lives and could no more run up a seam than cut a dress." Paris, of course, has so many wonderful work-people that it doesn't matter. Tell me, frankly: suppose a young woman dropped down at your feet between sunshine and showers from the sky, naked as God made her—to what extent could you dress her all by yourself?'

'From head to feet,' he cries emphatically. 'I learned to sew like a *cousette*. I had a strange adolescence, and came to Paris in search of work. Fate marched me straight to Augusta Bernard, and I learned to sew with the girls right from the humblest stages. I did it because I loved it. Augusta Bernard was in the class of great women designers—Mesdames Vionnet, Lanvin, and Chanel, possibly the greatest women dressmakers of the century.

'Am I married? No. It would be very difficult to be married in this profession. It is a profession unlike any other. What great artists have I dressed? I do not like that sort of question. I have no need to make capital out of my clients, but I believe that Véra Korène is your neighbour and that you are friends. There is a woman I love to dress.'

'I love her also,' I exclaim. 'She is going to Lyons this evening.'

'My policy is different from that of some great

dressmakers. Many seek sensationalism. They are
not altogether wrong. Their daring innovations bring
their names into the news, and in effect they merely do
what the Austrian vineyard owner does when he ties a
bunch of fir branches to the end of a pole and fastens it
to his garden gate, to show that he has some of the new
season's wine to sell. The danger with sensationalism
is that what hits the newspapers is often not becoming
to the woman. There is a serious conflict of interest
here, and a danger that to further your own ends you
may sacrifice good taste. I remain stubbornly outside
the bright lights, and try always to embellish with
simplicity the woman who comes to me.

'But I repeat there is no news in this sort of thing.
Of course, I can dress a woman much more successfully
if she is happy and in love.'

'In that case,' I say, laughing, 'we women would have
to have a man's freedom to fly from flower to flower
like a bee.'

'It would be better,' he agrees thoughtfully, 'for a
woman to have the courage to love as her heart dictates,
rather than to persecute a husband whom she no longer
loves.'

'My girl friends and I have spent the afternoon discussing the merits of slimming. We want to know if
it is worth it.'

'A thousand times,' he answers, 'and just as much for
a man as for a woman. Is it not our duty to retain an
agreeable outer form? A doctor fights against disease:
so we should battle against anything that makes us less
pleasing in appearance. A *couturier* would be foolish to
combat woman's desire to look slim. He must also be
the first to seize upon the amazing new textiles that the
scientists produce every year. They are without exception beautiful and will never do any harm to real
silk and wool.

'Am I superstitious? Nobody is so sure of himself that he has not a streak of superstition. Thus I always give my shows on a Tuesday. My father liked Tuesdays, and I adored my father. I have a little yellowed photograph of him in his Austrian uniform during the First World War which I must show you. Look! This was in the days of our glorious Austrian Empire. Yes, I have adopted Tuesday as my special day—and it has been kind to me. I was born on a Christmas night, just outside Vienna.'

'Do you get fond of the models you create?'

'When I am ready to show them I am terrified of them. If, two years later, they have proved successful, I love them. No, I do not model hats. I consider that this is the privilege of the milliner, just as a baker should leave the making of cakes to a pastry-cook.

'We are busy enough as it is keeping up with changing thought. Do not let people decry our age to you. Remember that what we admire in the past is always the pick of the basket: the lesser things, in fashions, in books, in paintings, in poetry, in music, turn to particles of forgotten dust. The giants remain and dazzle us. There are giants with us now, giants all about us. We must be young enough and clear-sighted enough to see them. Look at this lovely drawing by Dufy—Dufy, the great master, who made such lovely designs for textiles, Dufy who has only just gone to join Kisling and the other geniuses of his age.'

CHAPTER XXIV

M. JEAN-JACQUES GUERLAIN tells me that his father, who is a great lover and collector of pictures, does not entirely share my enthusiasm for Utrillo, and wants me to see the masterpieces that hang in the family home where all the Guerlains were born. So Jean-Jacques comes to fetch me in his car.

This magnificent house in the rue Murillo, whose existence one would never suspect from the street, because it is hidden behind a courtyard, looks out at the back on to the beautiful Parc Monceau, so that the view from this side surpasses anything that could be obtained from a private garden. An Alsatian dog welcomes us in the hall.

Mme Guerlain, who is not only a mother but also a grandmother, emerges from her drawing-room. Jean-Jacques kisses her respectfully. She smiles and says: 'Bonjour, mon grand!'

She is tall, stately, and elegant. Her lovely grey hair is twisted into a bun, and she wears a double row of superb black pearls, though black is an inadequate description for the green and rose tints that suggest the mysterious depths of tropical seas. Her skirt is grey: so also are her silk blouse and scarf. As a mother she is dignified, but as a grandmother she is amazingly young-looking, for her features are soft and pleasing. I am full of admiration. I reflect that the passing years have merely added to her beauty. I look at the pictures which are pointed out to me, but my eyes keep on turning to Mme Guerlain, for I think how splendid it would be to grow old like her.

Here is a Pissarro bathed in light, a landscape with fine trees, but the room in which we are standing is even more luminous, and through the open windows sunshine streams in, sunshine after showers, sunshine picking out the different greens of lawns and trees, and the brightly dressed children playing in the park. 'The sunshine is very welcome,' says Mme Guerlain. 'A wet spring is so discouraging for the dressmaking houses. I have bought a very pretty light summery dress, but I am still waiting for an opportunity to wear it. Now you must come and see the drawing-room.'

The furniture is period, which does not prevent a sofa on which Mme Récamier might have looked languidly beautiful from being occupied by two poodles which spring up and bark with joy at our arrival. This is a museum in which people live. Dogs and children enliven inanimate things as in the days when craftsmen made masterpieces for families in their homes. In the dining-room is a magnificent Van Gogh. There are a Reynolds and a Lawrence. These walls so richly hung could tell charming stories, stories of a family enriching itself in trade. One senses a century or more of laughter and tears.

I am being greatly honoured. These French families do not like strangers peeping within their doors, and one is surprised to discover how they blend austerity with great wealth. They have learned through various phases of French history—Charles X, Louis Philippe, Napoleon III, the Third Republic—to surround themselves with the beautiful and the fabulous. Their families have been ennobled by hard work, and they are neither ashamed of their work nor their wealth.

'Why yes,' Gérard Boucheron, who is of the same *milieu*, says to me later when I tell him about my fabulous visit. 'Why yes, Mme Guerlain has never quite ceased to intimidate me. I remember as a little boy being taken to see her, and I was very shy and frightened.'

I am lunching with Monick and Gérard Boucheron in the very modern apartment where they had given their cocktail-party a week earlier, and at which I had first met Jean-Jacques Guerlain.

On the occasion of the cocktail-party, their dining-room had been transformed to accommodate an enormous buffet. These elegant cocktail-parties in Paris have little in common with those in London. People who can still afford it think no champagne or food too expensive for the guests whom they ceremoniously receive on the threshold of their homes. They continue, in contrast to London, to keep up the same sumptuous hospitality as before the war. I had found much the same thing a few months earlier in Vienna, in spite of the presence of the Russians and the ruined state of the city.

This lunch, during which I speak of my visit to the Guerlains, is restfully quiet, but the roast fowl is sufficiently delicious to be commented on, and it transpires that Gérard has brought it back from Sologne where he has spent the week-end with his brother Fred. Monick wears a navy blue tailor-made which I greatly admire, though she confesses it is four years old.

We take coffee in the drawing-room. Once again the weather has turned to rain. Gérard shows us a diamond necklace which is not yet finished. The stones are set in wax, and this makes them look like stars in a midnight blue sky. 'Thus,' he explains, 'we can see exactly what the effect will be when the diamonds are set in platinum, and if we so desire we can, at this stage, alter the design, adding new stones or taking some away. This sort of jewel is generally made for a young married woman out of family heirlooms,

P

and we try to set out the stones to their best advantage. This, as you may guess, requires as much thought as the design of a beautiful dress. The diamonds themselves are generally all different in size and shape. Our first step, therefore, is to wrench them out of their old settings, after the manner of burglars, an operation requiring minute control. You have, I think, already seen our workmen wearing leather aprons to catch the shavings and dust, but even so it occasionally happens that some particle will escape the leather, and so the floor is swept at the end of each day, and the dust sifted.'

Gérard will talk for hours about the art of the diamond-setter and the pearl-stringer, and Monick, who knew nothing about these things at the beginning of her marriage, is now becoming quite an expert, capable of judging the size and colour of a diamond with great accuracy. In this connection I recall what the Begum Aga Khan once said to me in London, when I admired the way she received her husband's religious followers: 'But, my dear Madeleine, there is nothing one cannot learn if one applies oneself sufficiently.'

Gérard slips the diamond-studded wax into his brief-case and disappears.

Monick takes me to see her children. Chantal, the little girl, has a sore throat and will not go out to-day. She will play with her doll, but her mother promises to take her on at canasta after tea. Alain, the boy, will go for a walk in the Bois de Boulogne. Thus, though the children live in Paris, they enjoy the amenities of the country.

I accompany Monick to her bedroom and watch her put on the most adorable hat. She is a young woman of fashion, but works very hard to keep her home comfortable, and as she is essentially tidy, she lays down a strict routine for the servants, so that her household may be impeccably run during her journeys abroad, for she accompanies her husband on all his business trips. Thus, since her marriage, she has crossed many oceans and continents. The treasures of the Arabian Nights are Gérard's business, the wonders of Egypt, Persia, and India, and he derives great joy from initiating the young woman he loves into a kaleidoscope of new and romantic sights. The couple appear to be unusually fortunate, for they are young, good-looking, wealthy, and engrossed in an occupation that delights them.

'If only you knew, Madeleine,' exclaims Monick suddenly, 'how adorable Gérard is to me! His constant thought is to discover something fresh to enchant me. There are days when I wonder if I am not living in a dream.

'However, I have young women friends who seem just as happy. Jean-Jacques Guerlain's wife, for instance. Hers is a supremely successful marriage. He is immensely good-looking and very attentive to her. She is a wonderful friend to me, the sort of friend who is always thinking up ways of being kind. They have two children. On the children's birthdays, Jean-Jacques sends her immense baskets of flowers to thank her for having given him these children. Is there not something very lovely about this? Is it not a beautiful thing for a husband, on the children's birthdays, to think first about the wife, and to express his thanks? We are very fortunate to be happy in marriage.'

Monick puts on her gloves, takes up her bag, and continues:

'On my return from Spain where my husband and I spent a short time recently, I was surprised not to find my maid, for whom I have a great affection, waiting for me. She is young and I have trained her with care, and unlike most maids she does not spend her time telling me what her former mistresses did. She is willing to adapt herself to my tastes. Learning that she was in hospital, I went immediately to visit her, where to my immense surprise I found her with a baby.

'During all the months of her confinement, I had noticed nothing. I simply could not believe it. I, a woman, had not noticed that another woman, always in attendance on me, was pregnant! I must have been blind. I was not once aware of her discomfort or of her anguish, and she never excused herself from work.

'The baby was very sweet. She loved it, and so did I. My husband and I succeeded in placing the child in an excellent home, a very lovely place where I still go to see it, but I was terrified that my little maid would suddenly start to hate me or take a violent dislike to my own children. I feared she might envy my happiness, for I had a husband and an establishment of my own, whereas she had neither—but no, she continued to all appearances, to love me as well as, if not better than, before. Nevertheless, I am a trifle dubious and keep reminding myself that if she could be pregnant so long without my noticing it, I am perhaps not sufficiently observant to find out what she secretly thinks about me now.'

We are in the garage below the building. The tenants have ample room for their cars, and there is a turn-table which swivels round the moment one jams on the brakes. Monick uses her car as another woman might pick up her bag or her umbrella. It is raining hard and we feel very snug driving through the streets of Paris on our way to Givenchy, the *couturier*, who occupies a very fine house near the Parc Monceau. I am introduced to him but it is too late in the season for me to see the collection. Monick meets many of her girl friends who are either customers or who work in the establishment, but we decide that there is no point in staying any longer at Givenchy's, and we go to the

Pavillon de Marsan where there is an amazing exhibition of stained glass removed at the beginning of the war from the various cathedrals of France, and which will soon be put back where it belongs.

Here is the stained glass from Rouen Cathedral, which was so grievously and uselessly damaged by allied air bombardment. There are some fine windows also from the cathedrals of Bourges and Chartres.

The next morning, my friend Mr X, with whom I went to the races at Longchamp, telephones me while I am still in bed.

'What are you planning for to-day?' he asks.

'I ought to do some work,' I answer guardedly.

'I do not believe you,' he says. 'Now, let me consult my engagement book. I have a great number of cocktail-parties which I simply cannot miss, and a fantastically elegant ball at which there are sure to be some extraordinary women. I doubt if I shall go to bed before morning.'

Mr X's voice quivers at the thought of so much delight. The Paris season is honey to him. He laughs and asks me again about my plans.

'You are the only woman in Paris to whom I can telephone at such an early hour,' he declares. 'The others are either asleep till lunch-time or are hurrying off to work. This morning I am taking part in a golf tournament, and at one o'clock I must lunch at my club, but at three I shall call for you in my car.'

His car is of English make, but he drives it furiously in the continental manner. He skids through traffic, takes every risk, darts under the lights as they turn from green to red, and is an expert at jamming on the brakes at the last possible moment. Between social engagements he finds time to drive me all over Paris, and continually exclaims:

'Is any city in the world as beautiful as this?

'My heart bleeds every time I am obliged to leave it, and the older I grow, the less I want to travel. Rome is the only other capital I would occasionally trouble to visit, for Rome has true beauty, but beauty in itself is insufficient. Beauty is tinged with melancholy, whereas a man needs to laugh and to talk. Paris is the only city where gaiety and conversation have reached perfection. Its people are more intelligent and less proud than elsewhere.'

I listen indulgently to this man who is in love with his own town and, though my tastes are more international, I obtain considerable enjoyment from these exhilarating drives in his car. We cross and re-cross the Seine. We pass from crowded, narrow streets into wide avenues. Mr X asks me if I have ever noticed that the trees in the Avenue Henri-Martin embrace one another at the top, and he adds:

'Only winter will unclasp them!'

A moment later we stop behind another car which is held up by the traffic lights. It is a two-seater, and the young couple inside take advantage of this interlude to indulge in a long and passionate kiss. The lights change from red to green, but the lovers are too engrossed in their love-making to notice it. We hoot loudly. The lovers spring apart and the young man lets in the clutch, and their car darts ahead. As we overtake them, they turn and smile at us, and we smile back. Love is written all over their faces, and they are agreeable to look at, the boy good-looking, the girl pretty. We decide that they were justified in holding up the traffic. Mr X says:

'It was not chivalrous of me to hoot so imperiously, but I wanted to look at the girl. There is something intriguing about a young woman who has just been kissed. One wants to discover if she was worth it, but she *was* worth it, was she not? She was really very pretty.'

'*He* was good-looking,' I answer.

Mr X glances at me in surprise. He then breaks into laughter.

'I never thought there could be anything worth noticing in the young man,' he declares.

CHAPTER XXV

FROM THE apartment next to mine now comes a male voice, and I judge its owner to be a young but already important business man. He is telephoning to his wife at Evian. She is certainly elegant and he is clearly very much in love. A baby is expected in the autumn, and he expresses his joy at the thought that this happy event will take place while the grapes are being gathered. Do they live amongst vineyards? He is very anxious to join his wife but says that he must first fly to London. He has business there this afternoon. From London he will fly to Geneva whence a car will take him to Evian. I picture him as a modern Icarus soaring over the Eiffel Tower, skimming the channel, alighting in Piccadilly Circus, before the long final flight to Geneva to join the elegant wife who is expecting a baby when the grapes in the vineyards turn golden and ripe.

I ring for breakfast. Once a week I am served by Boris, the head floor-waiter, who is a White Russian, a very distinguished-looking person with greying hair and the sallow complexion peculiar to his race. He has fine manners, speaks the most exquisite French, and occasionally brings me my letters. I met him the other day in the corridor, and he said:

'Madame, a telegram has just come for you. You will find it on your dressing-table. I put it there with my own hands.'

I saw it as soon as I opened the door, placed at a coy angle against the mirror, and it struck me that Boris must be very chivalrous and attentive to women.

The coffee he brings me is piping hot. The milk roll is just out of the oven, but this I give to the sparrows who are already chirruping on the window ledge. Then, instinctively, I look across the slates to another window at which every morning a girl appears wearing a pink, a green, or a sky-blue apron. She generally steps out on to her little balcony and hangs some washing on a short line. She is very pretty and her blonde head bobs up and down level with the cord. I have come to look upon her as a living barometer. If the weather is set fair and sunshine is on the way, out comes the washing. When there are rain clouds, the washing is quickly hauled down. Her washing is as pleasant to look at as her own pretty head. The napkins are very gay and I always know what coloured apron she will wear on the morrow, for it is the first thing she hangs out on the cord to dry.

Émile Boss has been telling me more about the staff canteen. I did not at first realize that it had its own cooks. I am immensely intrigued about this side of the great organization over which I live, and now Émile tells me that the canteen cooks want me to come down and lunch with them. I am delighted.

We lunch at two, but the chefs are so busy looking after their staff colleagues that this is the earliest that they can sit down to their own meal. Their dining-room is beside the kitchen and has a long table over which presides M. Plantard, the head cook, who is a Burgundian. I am introduced. He introduces me in turn to M. Colin, *chef de partie*, from the Bresse, a part of the country famous for its fowls; M. Morère, *premier commis*; Kenneth Longbottom, a young Englishman learning the business in Paris; and Wichosky, the Polish dish-washer.

We waste no time in trivialities but break immediately

into red-hot discussion. My hosts have themselves cooked the meal that lies so temptingly in front of us. There is a great dish of warm young artichokes to be eaten as *hors-d'œuvre* with a *sauce vinaigrette*, and an enormous *omelette aux fines herbes et aux petits lardons*. Long French loaves lie in wicker baskets, and there is as much wine as anybody can drink.

M. Plantard fought in the First World War. He is now an elderly bachelor and walks home every evening with his pockets full of kitchen scraps which he distributes to stray cats who wait for him along the pavement, and who exist on his prodigality. He likes dogs and birds well enough but cats are his passion. I am inquisitive to know if this bachelor has any other hobbies besides feeding cats. What does a bachelor do all by himself in the evenings? Does he watch television?

'Television vexes me,' he says, 'because the tiny figures on the screen speak with such loud voices. The art of the chef lies in accurate dosage. Too much of one thing destroys a perfect balance. That is why TV vexes me.'

M. Morère is married, and likes to take his wife to the opera. He books his seats well in advance and they must be the very best in the house. A senior cook makes enough money these days to sit in the stalls beside millionaires who live at the Plaza-Athénée. When a man's work is done, says M. Morère, there must be no class distinction. He started by buying a house in the suburbs but he was so tired by the time he got home that he invariably went straight to bed. That was no life, he says. So he sold his house and moved to the centre of Paris. Now he goes to the opera and to the Comédie Française, and perhaps, from time to time, to a fashionable first night. Life has become exciting.

M. Colin, on the other hand, likes to listen on the radio to the Scala in Milan, but he is in no hurry to

get a television set, thinking it more important to buy
a refrigerator. This opinion meets with general assent.
We then talk about herbs, and I ask M. Plantard if
garlic, so laughed at by foreigners, is used in the food
cooked in luxury hotels.

'Yes,' he answers. 'The only trouble with garlic is
that so few people know how to use it. They cook the
cloves without first crushing them. You must not
take liberties with condiments and spices. Better too
little than too much.'

Émile Boss tells us that he has struggled since boyhood against the handicap of having only one arm. One
senses in his every phrase a stern will to succeed. M.
Plantard and he worked together at the Hôtel George V
during the German occupation—M. Plantard in the
kitchens, M. Boss in the stores. Every day M. Boss
watched Field Marshal von Rundstedt walking down the
Champs Élysées alone, his hands clasped behind his back,
his eyes scanning the shop windows. The spectacle of
the Champs Élysées charmed him. These Germans
loved Paris, and I am surprised to note with what
complete absence of rancour most Parisians speak of
them. Old scores, as it were, have been wiped clean.
These Germans, one hears, were civilized. They
appreciated good food, succumbed to the charms of
intelligent conversation, and were nice enough to adore
Paris!

Émile Boss is the son of a clog-maker in the Auvergne,
which was formerly famed for its artisans. Life was
hard, however, and after the death of his father, Émile,
still a lad, came to Paris where his uncle sold fish. He
said he would tell us a story about this period of his
life for the sake of M. Plantard who liked animals.
One day a mongrel followed his uncle in the street,
and would not be driven off. So his uncle took the
animal home.

'That evening my uncle was too busy to take much notice of the dog, which came and went as it pleased,' says M. Boss, 'but when my uncle was counting his till, his eyes suddenly fell on a shoulder of lamb at the side of it, and as we were poor, he flew into a great rage, demanding that he should be immediately informed which of us had gone to this extravagance. As nobody would own up, my uncle accused us of lying.

'The next evening when my uncle was again counting his till he saw in the same place—three beautiful peaches!

'We soon discovered that the mongrel we were befriending had stolen these things and placed them there for my uncle to find. The dog had been trained by his previous master to thieve from shops and was merely continuing a profession learned in puppyhood. He had come to the conclusion that as my uncle was the head of our family, the neighbourhood of the till was the proper place for depositing the booty. He had doubtless been separated in the crowded street from his previous master and now rendered the same type of service to the new one. The next day we followed him and saw him slink to the back of a greengrocer's stall, where with incredible skill he knocked down half a dozen tomatoes which he stealthily brought back, one by one, to the accustomed hiding-place, carrying them so gently between his teeth that the fruit showed no sign of bruising. My uncle beat him savagely to cure him of his evil habits, and we kept him with us for fourteen years.'

I ask M. Plantard a question, the answer to which I am longing to know. Does he feel it less glamorous to cook for the staff than for the famous people who patronize the hotel?

'Not at all,' he answers quickly. 'The whole idea of the new France is that the country's finest chefs should

be available for the employees. The servant is as
worthy as his master. This post holds advantages for
the cook who is no longer young, for there is not the
mad rush that at certain hours reduces the main kitchens
of an hotel to pandemonium.'

Émile Boss, whose eyes are shining, says with a true
sense of democracy:

'I am very proud of my chefs. They are great
masters. By humbling themselves, they have in my
opinion gone up in the world!'

It is as if the man's entire philosophy were contained
in these words.

Great bowls of Chantilly cream are now placed in
front of us. Here is a dish few women can manage
successfully in their homes. We can never reach the
heights of male cooking.

'That is true,' says M. Plantard to whom I make this
confession, 'but tastes have changed enormously and the
grande cuisine no longer exists. No restaurant is asked
for the complicated dishes of yesterday. A grilled
steak is what people call for to-day. Meals are becoming lighter. In the days of my apprenticeship there
was a soup called Crème Crécy. Two of us were needed
to crush the carrots, though we only used the softer
parts, throwing the hearts away. Fresh farm cream was
added, and the result was as smooth as velvet. Nobody
to-day would dream of asking for this soup: conversely
only men of my age would know how to make it. I
agree that in the old days menus were rather long. One
continually saw dishes sent back to the kitchen scarcely
touched. On the other hand it is sad to see men discard
the cunning of their trade.'

Jeanne is lunching by herself at the Relais, and I have
promised to meet her for coffee. This fine buttery
which never closes and which, translated into English,

means the place where stage-coaches change horses, is the rendezvous for actors and actresses, dress designers and mannequins, playwrights, diplomats, and visitors from all over the world.   In Paris places like this are busy all round the clock.   Ali, whose black face and hands emerge from magnificent robes, arrives with his coffee-making utensils.   His smile is more than usually beatific, for he is wearing his royal blue uniform which, according to Jeanne, is certainly as fine as those made for elegant Spahi officers, with the result, says Jeanne, that his beautiful robes must have cost as much as she or I would have to pay for an exclusive model from Balmain or Dior!

I share her jealousy, and think darkly how nice it would be to order myself a new cocktail dress from the most expensive *couturier* in Paris, but Jeanne, who is by nature far too gay to brood, has turned her attention to a party of Americans laughing at a nearby table. She says that one of the most curious things about seeing foreigners at play is that it is hard to imagine them in their own countries, in an atmosphere of anxiety and hard work.

'When my husband and I were passing through New York on our way to Mexico,' she says, 'we received invitations from a great many people with whom we had become friendly here. I love the Americans and looked forward to seeing as many as possible in their homes. There were two men in particular who asked us to telephone them at their club as soon as we arrived. We had, of course, only seen them at play. I could not imagine them in any other role. They were as carefree as the people at the table opposite. Well, my husband and I went to their club. One of them took his hat and coat, the other led us to the best table and then stood over us with the menu. They owned the club, one of the most exclusive in New York, but they worked round the clock, and were not ashamed to be seen with napkins over their arms, taking the orders, rushing out into the kitchen. So I realized that the people whom we see at play in Paris work just as we do when they go back to New York.'

I like Jeanne's story, and I suddenly think of M. Morère, the *premier commis* in the staff kitchen, untying his apron at the end of the day and taking his wife to the most expensive seats at the Opera House, so that he may rub shoulders with the famous while he listens to the tunes of Offenbach.

These are the advantages of a changing world.

CHAPTER XXVI

MY FRIEND Mr X, seated at a desk in the hall, is studying a book of racing form. He must find a winner, he says, looking up at my approach, because lately he has been right out of luck. He assures me that the fault is with the horses which are no good at all this year. Seeing my interest and surprise, he breaks out laughing.

One might be forgiven for supposing that Mr X never does any work. That is far from the case, but he deals in raw materials, in jute and cotton, with the result that there are certain months in the year when he works in a perfect frenzy, rushing from Liverpool to Belfast, and from Marseilles to Cairo, hardly sleeping, not even bothering to lunch—then in early summer while the jute and cotton are being turned into finished products, Mr X plays with the same enthusiasm as earlier he worked.

'To-day,' he declares, 'it is imperative that I should be seen watching polo, but I am not allowed to take you into the grounds. Would you mind terribly if I left you in the car like a lapdog?'

I tell him that I shall be perfectly happy dreaming under the trees in the Bois de Boulogne, and that indeed I would much prefer this to walking endlessly round a polo field. He looks at me suspiciously and answers:

'It is not natural for a woman to be so accommodating.'

I smile and decide that it is not worth pointing out that a woman is invariably accommodating with a man who is not her husband.

The Bois de Boulogne is at its loveliest. Sunshine has once again followed rain, and trees and grass contrast their verdure. There are many magnificent cars parked outside the polo grounds, and Mr X exclaims that he ought to have arrived half an hour earlier. 'Everybody who matters will be here,' he adds in a burst of egoistical candour. 'It will be a wonderful sight.'

He manages to park his small English car between two enormous Cadillacs and then, so self-conscious and vain are men, prepares a fitting entry into this exclusive club. He opens his cigar case, chooses a cigar, and looks round for something with which to pierce it, but in his fluster, fearing that he may be watched, pulls out his gold pencil and makes the hole with the lead point; but he has no sooner put the cigar between his lips than they are dyed bright blue. I show him the result in the mirror of my flapjack. He swears terribly but I am so doubled up with laughter that he ends by laughing also.

'A cigar is *de rigueur*,' he confesses with childlike simplicity. 'It makes one look so very Jockey Club!'

He repairs the damage, and I watch him disappear.

A number of really beautiful women wearing very large hats make their appearance. Their dresses from the greatest houses in Paris are superb. Many have been obliged to park their cars so far away that they appear to have arrived on foot. Their very high heels sink into the sandy path. There is too much wind for hats so large. Nevertheless they make a fine picture. The men are elegant too, but there are far more women than men.

I am suddenly deliriously happy to breathe the pure, sweet air of the Bois de Boulogne. I feel perfectly relaxed. The car is very comfortable. I am neither too hot nor too cold, and though I am wearing very high heels, my feet do not hurt. I can criticize other

Q

women without being criticized myself. I run no risk of my hat blowing off. The minutes fly. I watch the glory of the Bois without thinking about anything in particular.

Suddenly I hear horses' hoofs and wheels. Here comes a fine equipage, the coachman very erect, whip in hand. Beside him, even more erect, sits a young lady of twelve or thirteen, dressed in an impeccably cut riding-habit, the daughter of some wealthy family, taught at this early age to remain in dignified silence beside the servant who is driving her.

Two other equipages arrive from the opposite direction, and now four, six, eight, horses are all stamping and wheeling in the avenue, the noise of their hoofs and the jingling of the harness deadening the sound of passing cars. What a terrifying sight it must have been in the old days to see a coach out of control, the runaway horses thundering away till coach and passengers were overturned in a ditch! The grooms have taken their places and one, who is wearing a *chéchia*, looks very fine.

Here are three riders dressed in scarlet with black velvet caps. They are galloping in close formation and I watch in fascination their supple bodies rise and drop rhythmically. At the entrance to the wood, without slackening speed, they separate and I see them pass like phantoms between the trees. Now the wood has swallowed them up. Now a speck of scarlet splashes black trunk or green bough. The three riders came into my vision and passed out of it with the speed of a dream.

I am in the front of the car, my arm resting against the open window frame. My mind is full of these enchanting scenes. Suddenly I hear a voice:

'I say, lady, please lady, do you speak English?'

Involuntarily I jump in my seat. Why am I so nervous? Was I dreaming or am I really in the Bois? An American soldier is leaning out of the cab of an enormous truck. Another G.I. is seated beside him. Their blue eyes are turned appealingly in my direction.

'Lady, do you speak English?'

'Why yes. Of course I speak English.'

They break into delighted smiles. They want me to direct them to the American Hospital, for they have lost their way in the wood and cannot find their way out.

Alas, we speak the same language but I am not able to help them. I am myself lost in the immensity of these fields and trees and feel like Little Red Riding Hood. The two G.I.s are crestfallen. They were so sure that I could help them. Suddenly I see an old lady and an old gentleman walking sedately along the avenue in our direction. The gentleman is very elegant and wears a light suit and a Panama. The lady wears a black tailor-made, but she has a string of pearls and the jabot of her blouse is of white lace. As soon as they come level with us, I lean out of the other window and inquire if they can direct my two G.I.s to the American Hospital.

'Oh,' exclaims the lady in a delighted voice, 'my husband will be honoured to direct them. Just consider, madame, that he was liaison officer with THEM during the First World War. Yes, dear madame, with the first American army to land in France. He speaks admirable English.'

The old gentleman, who suddenly looks twenty years younger, has hurried into the middle of the avenue where he stands looking up at the G.I.s in the truck. His directions are splendidly concise. His wife who has remained beside me confesses that her husband simply adores to speak English. The truck gives a great roar and thunders away. The old gentleman gazes in the direction which it has taken, as if its disappearance has left an emptiness in his heart. He then turns to me and takes off his hat and bows, politely but without undue

warmth.   The lady smiles at me in a cold, distant way.
I sense that they would not easily invite me into their
home—and yet how kind they were to the G.I.s!

The car behind me, in trying to get out into the
avenue, has pushed into our bumpers and thrown me
violently forward, but never mind, here is Mr X, all
smiles.

'Dear lady,' he exclaims, 'you have no idea how elegant the polo was to-day.   My appearance was a tremendous success.   I was noticed by all the smartest
people in Paris.   The ladies had beautiful dresses and
I must have kissed a hundred pretty hands!   I simply
love to see women with big hats.   I do hope you have
not been too bored?'

'Not at all,' I answer.   'I saw three young men in
scarlet galloping into the wood, and two charming
Americans stopped to talk to me.'

'Oh!' he says, a little vexed.

'And now you must drive me quickly back to Paris,'
I said, 'for I am invited to an important cocktail-party.'

The party is at the beautiful house where the two little
girls invited their friends to a birthday tea, but this
time we shall all be grown-ups.   I hurry up to my
apartment to slip on my blue foulard dress, and when I
come down again Mr X, who is waiting for me in the
Relais, admits that I am looking my best.   I know that
he is telling the truth.

He drives me to the rue de Berri and leaves me at the
courtyard of the great house where police are already
directing the flow of cars.   I am excited, but a little
put out that I shall have to climb the steps all by myself.
I have no cigar, like Mr X, to give me a countenance.
One needs to be a very brave woman to enter a crowded
salon alone.   For a brief moment I wish frantically that
I were Véra Korène!

CHAPTER XXVII

BORIS HAS brought me another telegram. I must fly back to London this afternoon. What shall I take with me? Ought I to do any packing? I move restlessly about my attic putting things in my dressing-case, taking them out again. I have a sudden vision of all the women who arrive on my corridor with immense trunks in which their dresses can stand up on hangers. I cannot bear travelling with luggage. The very idea of packing puts me in a panic. I shall make a parcel of some of the things I shall need in Normandy this summer and send it by post. A single attaché case will suffice for my journey to London.

I take my parcel to the post office in the rue Clément Marot. As it is Saturday and the sun is shining, the girls behind the counter are all in cotton dresses, and they look like a page in colour in my favourite women's magazine. The man in front of me asks for a telephone call to Cairo, and the girl in her light dress writes down the number without any of the emotion that overcomes me at the sound of this distant capital. She is probably much too excited about her own week-end. Perhaps her young man will take her to pick lilac in the woods outside Paris.

I dispatch my parcel of summer frocks to my mother in Normandy and emerge into this district of Paris which I like to think of as my own. I look down the street as if I were afraid never to see it again—a police-station, a milk shop where they sell thick country cream and all sorts of wonderful cheeses, a fruiterer whose goods are protected by a large fisherman's net, and a chemist whose window is flanked by tall mirrors. These mirrors are my best friends. A glance in their direction when I trot down the street tells me if I must cut out those tempting strawberry tarts which at this time of year appear at the end of every meal.

I call on Georges, my shoemaker, who has been mending the heels of all my shoes, even of those I did not buy from him. I have become so accustomed to wearing the tapering high heels that I feel quite miserable without them.

'To think that this evening I shall be walking down Piccadilly!' I confide to Georges. He says: '*Bon voyage*, little madame!' and I go out into the sunshine again where I bend down to stroke the large, black cat of a nearby apartment house. He is not very friendly but his owners adore him. They have a ground-floor window ledge with flowers and three saucers for the cat—one containing milk, the second water, and the third freshly cut meat. A little girl is playing on the sidewalk. She is dressed gipsy fashion with a very long, wide skirt and a yellow kerchief over her head. I inquire how old she is and she answers very proudly that she is six.

'Your gipsy costume suits you very well.'

'Ah,' she exclaims, fixing me with her large eyes.

'But you must feel rather hot with the shawl crossed over your shoulders?'

'Oh no, madame!' she exclaims.

She does not feel the heat because her gipsy costume suits her and she is a girl. I smile at her understandingly. There is a shop next door where they sell little squares of coloured silk on which the letters that make up the word PARIS are scattered in bright and picturesque confusion. One folds these squares in a certain manner, and then one is supposed to fasten them round the neck with the help of a double ring so that the silk is not crushed. The result is quite enchanting, and I decide to buy a number of them for my friends in London and New York. I am also shown some ties of brightly coloured foulard: 'Yes, madame, like the ties gentlemen wear, but much gayer. You slip them under the collar of your blouse and tie a small bow under the chin. See, madame! Is not the effect charming? It makes all the difference to your tailor-made!'

Yes, indeed, it is charming. How curious! I was here only a week ago, and this novelty did not exist. Thus feminine fashion springs up in Paris from one day to the other, as flowers blossom out in a garden.

But I have made a discovery. A tie is very warm on a hot day. No wonder men are always so anxious to rid themselves of their ties. This is a fashion that would not please me after all.

We are in the middle of a heat-wave. I shall lunch quietly at the Relais like a person satisfied that her work is nearly finished. I was anxious this summer to write a book about Paris. I have accomplished what I set out to do. I like to live with intensity, not to give way to fatigue, not to rest. 'I live on my nerves,' said Véra Korène, 'with my heart, or with my brains. An actress should *never* relax.'

On my way through the foyer I meet Annie.

'Annie, come and have lunch with me.'

'I cannot,' she says, 'but I will join you for coffee.'

Jacques, the 'friend of Achilles,' smiles from behind his bookstall. He is surrounded by copies of the current *Elle*. All my women friends in Paris read *Elle* for the horoscope. The 'friend of Achilles' was born in August. This audacious man is a lion. I am a lioness. Véra Korène is a lioness.

I order a steak and a glass of champagne. Three extremely pretty women are lunching together at the table next to mine. One of them wears a navy blue dress made in the particular form of crochet-work that Anny Blatt made fashionable, and this interests me prodigiously, because when I was last in London, Katie, my London dressmaker, was making a crochet two-piece for her sister Millie, my milliner. I was anxious to do something of the same sort for myself, and now I am more than ever resolved to do so, for the young woman at the adjoining table is certainly most elegant. I must remember to watch her when she goes out to see if this crochet-work does not broaden the silhouette.

At another table a party of English people are talking about Manchester. A Spaniard and his son whom I often meet in the lift are lunching very quietly together, and they smile at me. The father was a close friend of King Alfonso. Here is Annie looking for me. I wave to her and she rushes across the room to say that she cannot take coffee with me after all but that here is Alex Maguy to take her place. M. Maguy sits down, accepts a glass of champagne, and tells me that he has come to take me to his apartment opposite Notre Dame so that I can see his pictures before I fly back to London.

As we reach the door, Alex Maguy whispers:

'There is a lady on your left calling you.'

I look round and at a corner table I see Ethel Linder Reiner looking magnificent in a dress cut low at the neck. Though she is in Paris her smartness is entirely American. Women of different nationalities retain, in spite of the speed of travel, their native style, and this is as it should be. Personally I think she looks wonderful, and I tell her so.

'Oh, thank you!' she exclaims sweetly. 'If you say so, I feel it must be true.'

She is in the middle of a business lunch. Playwrights and film producers have surrounded her since she arrived in Paris. Alex Maguy and I hurry through the foyer. Sunshine pours through the leafy trees of the Avenue Montaigne, and the air is dry and hot as in Spain. We cross the Pont Neuf, look down upon the scintillating waters of the Seine, the fishermen seated on the banks, and ten minutes later we reach the historic Quai des Orfèvres.

The house is very old, and there are four floors to be mounted without the aid of an elevator. The spiral staircase turns and turns. Maguy is as lithe as a cat but I am perched on heels far too high for this exercise, and my skirt is too narrow for the steep steps.

But how great is my reward when finally he leads me into the big airy room with its walls painted white and its wide balcony shaded by orange sun-blinds that diffuse a cool glow. In front of the wide-open window a table is laid for him alone. Pictures by modern masters radiate that spirit of youth and comradeship which I had noticed at his dressmaking house. Here, for instance, the canvases of Kisling seem wonderfully appropriate. This Viennese painter, French by assimilation, seems to mirror all that Maguy loves. Here is a fine canvas by Raoul Dufy who, like Kisling, was with us so short a time ago. 'They were my friends,' says Maguy simply. 'I have a record of Kisling's voice that makes me cry every time I play it on the phonograph. Listen!'

He plays the record and I hear a low voice without any trace of accent. What is he saying? That he is living just now in Provence, land of blue skies and olive-trees and soft, singing voices, land so beloved by painters because of the magnificent clarity of the light. The voice ceases and Maguy explains that his friend died at Cagnes.

'I was in Paris at the time,' he says. 'I was working on a collection. The moment I heard that he was ill I hurried to his side but it was too late. He was my foster-brother: we had the same wet-nurse just outside Vienna. So you see, when he died I really lost a brother.

'He had come to Paris before I did, and when I arrived fresh from Vienna he was already the famous "Kiki of Montparnasse." He was sweet-tempered, very patient, and a magnificent painter. Look! Between the canvases of Kisling and Dufy I have hung a Braque which, in spite of its brown tints, is as luminous as anything.'

What a strange and intriguing room! A short staircase leads up to his bedroom and a tiny bath-room in which hangs a magnificent drawing by Picasso. These upper galleries are so curiously designed that they give the impression of being a theatrical *décor*. There is a nude by Renoir, and now here I am leaning over the balustrade looking down into the big airy room with the Kislings, the Dufy, the Braque, a Utrillo, and a Matisse.

I inspect his bedroom with his divan cunningly placed against the wall, and under some rolls of material I discover a dressmaker's dummy which he says he brings out to work on when he cannot sleep, for his mind is always busy designing, planning forthcoming dress shows. There is a great bowl of ripe apricots diffusing the bright colours one associates with Van Gogh. We plunge our hands into the bowl and greedily taste the ripe, golden brown fruit.

The wide balcony is almost a suspended garden. Climbing roses garland the sides, entwine their branches round the wrought-iron bars. Below us the Seine flows serpent-like, and as in some impressionist painting we look down on the straw hat of a man fishing.

We continue to eat apricots, dropping the stones on anything that takes our fancy underneath, and from time to time our eyes turn in the direction of the Pont

Neuf, the oldest bridge in Paris on which the poet Baudelaire so often dreamed, rhyming his finest poems.

'Now,' says Maguy, taking my arm, 'lean a little to this side and you will see a tiny public garden, called the Jardin Henri IV, named after the king of France who more than any other loved and admired women. Fittingly this garden is mostly, I might say almost exclusively, frequented by young students who exchange therein the first kisses of adolescence. On the other side of the Seine lives Picasso when he is not in the Midi.'

The heat of this tropical day burns through us. The slowly moving water of the Seine throws up the green and rosy tints of Mme Guerlain's black pearls.

We return into the big room.

At the door of her kitchen stands Gabrielle, the cook. I think she is displeased with me because I have pre-vented her master from eating his lunch. She does not know that in a few hours I shall be in London. Maguy says to me:

'I came across Gabrielle in curious circumstances. Did I tell you that during the war I worked for a time in the *maquis* in Auvergne, and once when I was being hunted down by the Germans I saw Gabrielle standing in the courtyard of her own farm. I implored her to hide me. She made me her farm-hand and I worked for her all one summer, acting as her swineherd and helping to bring in the hay—and then after the war we exchanged roles. She left her farm and came to work for me. And now, like Renoir, I have my Gabrielle!'

Gabrielle smiles.

Her parents are looking after her farm, and this morning she has received from them a large smoked ham which she is anxious for us to taste. She has forgiven me, I fancy. We are going to be friends. She takes a long, sharp, narrow knife and using it against the ham, like a bow to a violoncello, she shaves off two delicious slices. We stand beside her, eating the ham from our fingers, but the clock ticks ominously and I must go. We say good-bye to Gabrielle and hurry down the four flights of stairs, but this time I take off my shoes and descend in my stockinged feet. I am wearing nylons and I fear no holes.

We cross the Pont Neuf, and I think of Baudelaire. The white stone burns in the fierce sun. Alex Maguy tells me that every evening he walks home from work along the quays. The *sergents de ville* all know him.

A taxi deposits me at the Plaza-Athénée. The porter has brought down my dressing-case. The aeroplane ticket is waiting for me. As usual, however, there are a number of objects for which there is no room in my case. Happily I have a string bag! I have never yet made a journey without having recourse to this inelegant adjunct which must give me the appearance of a woman returning from market. My friend Annie has brought me three adorable marguerites in white piqué snugly lying in a transparent box made of cellophane. I tenderly kiss Jeanne good-bye and ask her to look after the beautiful pink hydrangea I have left behind. And here, almost forgotten, is the copy of *She stoops to Conquer* which I bought from a box on the left bank of the Seine. I place it lovingly with the box of piqué marguerites in the string bag. My Oliver Goldsmith will thus return to its country of origin. *She stoops to Conquer* will speed with me through the azure sky of this tropical afternoon. I salute you, Mr Goldsmith. Who can say after this that fame has not wings!

DATE DUE
